The fairy tradition in the B varied one. *A Book of Fairies* celebrates this diversity with essays, poems and a wonderful selection of reported sightings and country tales, ranging from medieval chronicles to stories handed down almost within living memory. They are tales of things half-understood, things now-unreachable, things seen for an instant and gone.

Katharine Briggs, who died in 1980, was a British folklorist and President of the English Folklore Society as well as the author of a number of major works. Her great *A Dictionary of Fairies*, from which this anthology is drawn, is available in Penguin.

'Katharine Briggs is the magic mirror on the wall. Ask her what you will . . .'
        – Richard Adams

A Book of Fairies

KATHARINE BRIGGS

PENGUIN BOOKS

PENGUIN BOOKS

Published by the Penguin Group
Penguin Books Ltd, 27 Wrights Lane, London W8 5TZ, England
Penguin Books USA Inc., 375 Hudson Street, New York, New York 10014, USA
Penguin Books Australia Ltd, Ringwood, Victoria, Australia
Penguin Books Canada Ltd, 10 Alcorn Avenue, Toronto, Ontario, Canada M4V 3B2
Penguin Books (NZ) Ltd, 182–190 Wairau Road, Auckland 10, New Zealand

Penguin Books Ltd, Registered Offices: Harmondsworth, Middlesex, England

A Dictionary of Fairies first published by Allen Lane 1976
Published in Penguin Books 1977
This selection published under the title A Book of Fairies in Penguin Books 1997
1 3 5 7 9 10 8 6 4 2

Set in 10/13pt Monotype Sabon
Typeset by Rowland Phototypesetting Ltd, Bury St Edmunds, Suffolk
Printed in England by Clays Ltd, St Ives plc

Contents

Preface

The anthology is entirely taken from Katharine Briggs's great work *A Dictionary of Fairies*. This remarkable book draws together a lifetime's research into the folklore of the British Isles and is a treasure-chest of the beguiling, eerie and odd. The author's own definition of 'fairy' was extremely broad and for the purpose of this small book has been narrowed to only the 'little people' themselves (and the occasional gnome). Those wishing to read about giant worms, black dogs, the Roaring Bull of Bagbury or the appalling skriker will need to refer to the *Dictionary* itself.

The collection starts with a group of brilliant short essays on fairies by Katharine Briggs, but the great majority of the pieces gathered here consist simply of the fairy-lore itself – the extraordinary beliefs, reports, verses and country tales (some in dialect) which form such a haunting tradition throughout the British Isles. All the material is presented in as authentic a form as possible and carries a gripping sense of ancient custom, of long-believed rumour or of personal shock.

All references have been dropped as these are given in full in the *Dictionary*. The figure of the *Will o' the Wisp* which recurs throughout the book is taken from T. Crofton Croker's *The Fairy Legends and Traditions of the South of Ireland* (1826).

Essays on Fairies

The Origin of Fairies

Those inhabitants of Britain who used to believe in the fairies, and that small number who still believe in them, have various notions about their origin, and this variety is not purely regional but is partly founded on theological differences. Folklorists and students of fairy-lore who have not committed themselves to personal beliefs also put forth a selection of theories of fairy origins, which for the sake of clarity can be examined separately.

A valuable work of research on the beliefs held about fairy origins among the Celts was published by Evans Wentz under the title *The Fairy-Faith in Celtic Countries* (1911). In the course of his work he travelled in Ireland, the Highlands of Scotland, Wales, the Isle of Man, Cornwall and Brittany, interviewing first eminent scholars, such as Douglas Hyde in Ireland and Alexander Carmichael in the Highlands, and also people of all classes and types who were believed to have information about the fairies. He found that, among the older people, many of the opinions of the seventeenth and eighteenth centuries still prevailed.

There seemed to be some trace of the prehistoric beliefs left, though these were not so explicit as the beliefs in the fairies as the dead, or as fallen angels, or occasionally as astral or elemental spirits.

Sometimes the particular class of the dead is specified. The sluagh or fairy Hosts are the evil dead, according to Highland belief. Finvarra's following in Ireland seem to comprise the dead who have recently died as well as the ancient dead; but they are almost as sinister as the Sluagh. In Cornwall the small people are the souls of the heathen dead, who died before Christianity and were not good enough for Heaven nor bad enough for Hell, and therefore lingered on, gradually shrinking until they became as small as ants, and disappeared altogether out of the world. The fairy dwelling on Selena Moor gives a good account of this theory. In Cornwall and Devon too the souls of unchristened babies were called piskies, and appeared at twilight in the form of little white moths. The knockers in the tin mines were souls of the dead too, but of the Jews who had been transported there for their part in the Crucifixion. In Wales the belief in the fairies as the dead does not seem to have been so common. They were often described as a race of 'beings half-way between something material and spiritual, who were rarely seen', or 'a real race of invisible or spiritual beings living in an invisible world of their own' (Wentz, p. 145). In the Isle of Man a passage on the 'Nature of Fairies' is something the same:

'The fairies are spirits. I think they are in this country yet: A man below here forgot his cow, and at a late hour went to look for her, and saw that crowds of fairies like little boys were with him. (St) Paul said that spirits are thick in the air, if only we could see them; and we call spirits fairies. I think the old people here in the island thought of fairies in the same way.' [Wentz, p. 125]

The belief in the fairies as the dead may well come from pre-Christian times, but with the fairies as fallen angels we come into the post-Christian period. In Ireland, in spite of the lively belief in Finvarra and his host, there is also an explicit belief in the fairies as fallen angels. Lady Wilde contradicts the usual trend of her testimony in one chapter of her *Ancient Legends of Ireland* (vol. 1), 'The Fairies as Fallen Angels' (p. 169):

The islanders, like all the Irish, believe that the fairies are the fallen angels who were cast down by the Lord God out of heaven for their sinful pride. And some fell into the sea, and some on the dry land, and some fell deep down into hell, and the devil gives to these knowledge and power, and sends them on earth

5

where they work much evil. But the fairies of the earth and the sea are mostly gentle and beautiful creatures, who will do no harm if they are let alone, and allowed to dance on the fairy raths in the moonlight to their own sweet music, undisturbed by the presence of mortals.

From the Scottish Highlands, Evans Wentz (p. 85) quotes a lively account of the story behind this, given to him by Alexander Carmichael, who heard it in Barra in company with J. F. Campbell:

'The Proud Angel fomented a rebellion among the angels of heaven, where he had been a leading light. He declared that he would go and found a kingdom for himself. When going out at the door of heaven the Proud Angel brought prickly lightning and biting lightning out of the doorstep with his heels. Many angels followed him – so many that at last the Son called out, "Father! Father! the city is being emptied!" whereupon the Father ordered that the gates of heaven and the gates of hell should be closed. This was instantly done. And those who were in were in, and those who were out were out; while the hosts who had left heaven and had not reached hell flew into the holes of the earth, like the stormy petrels.'

The greater part of these angels were thought of, like the Cornish muryans, as 'too good for Hell and too bad for

Heaven', but with the growth of Puritanism the view of the fairies became darker and the fallen angels began to be regarded as downright devils, with no mitigating feature. We find this in seventeenth-century England. William Warner in *Albion's England* goes so far as to deny all performance of household tasks to Robin Goodfellow, saying ingeniously that he got the housewives up in their sleep to clean their houses. Robin got the credit of the work, and the poor housewife got up in the morning more tired than when she had gone to bed. This is to deprive the fairy character of all benevolence. On the other hand, two of the Puritan divines of the same period allow the fairies to be a kind of spiritual animal, of a middle nature between man and spirit. It is clear that there was no lack of diversity between those who believed in the real existence of fairies.

The Dress and Appearance
of Fairies

The fairies of Britain vary as much in dress as they do in appearance and size. Most people, asked off-hand about the colour of the fairies' clothes, would answer 'green' without hesitation, and they would not be far astray. Green is generally acknowledged to be the fairy colour, particularly in Celtic countries, and for this reason is so unlucky that many Scotswomen refuse to wear green at all. Red runs green very close, and in Ireland the small trooping fairies, the daoine sidh and the shefro, wear green coats and red caps while the solitary fairies, such as the lepracauns, the cluricaune and the fear dearg, generally wear red. William Allingham describes:

> Wee folk, good folk, trooping all together,
> Green jacket, red cap and white owl's feather.

This seems to be a typical costume of the small trooping fairies. The lil' fellas of Man, about three feet in height, are described by Sophia Morrison as wearing green coats and red caps, or occasionally leather ones on hunting expeditions. Their hunting dogs were of all fancy colours, green, blue, red. Red caps were very common for all kinds of the homelier fairies. Even the merrow in Crofton Croker's story wore a red cap to enable him to go through the sea to a dry land under it, and gave a similar one to his human friend, which had to be thrown back when he returned to land. Red, blue and white caps were used in various stories of fairy levitation. Grigs, little South Country fairies, wore red caps. A cluricaune of the abbey lubber type is described by Crofton Croker as wearing a red nightcap, a leather apron, long light-blue stockings and high-heeled, buckled shoes. Even the mourners at the fairy funeral in Bowker's *Goblin Tales of Lancashire*, though they were sombrely clad otherwise, wore bright red caps. The green-clad fairy ladies enjoyed a touch of red as much as the fairy men, but they introduced it in their slippers, like the little lady in 'The Fairies of Merlin's Crag' from Gibbings's *Folk-Lore and Legends, Scotland* who was eighteen inches high, with long golden hair hanging to her waist, a long green dress and red slippers. The tiny fairy gentleman who wooed Anne Jefferies was too much of a dandy to wear a red cap, but he brightened his green clothing by a red feather in his hat. In Somerset the fairies are said to wear red, and the rougher pixies green. This is the opposite way round to the Irish colour scheme. Elves wear green. Many of the Green Ladies of Scotland were connected with the dead, and so naturally wore green, for green is the Celtic colour of death. The silkies of the North of England generally wore glistening white silk, the white ladies of Man wore white satin, and the tylwyth teg of Wales wore white. Isobel Gowdie, the self-confessed witch who gave a vivid account of her traffic with the fairies, described the Fairy Queen rather prosaically: 'The Qwein of Fearrie is brawlie clothed in whyt linens, and in whyt and browne cloathes.' A Fairy Queen whose visit to a Galloway cottage is described in J. F. Campbell's *Popular Tales of the West Highlands* (vol. II, pp. 67–8) was more glamorous:

> She was very magnificently attired; her dress was of the richest green, embroidered round with spangles of gold, and on her head was a small coronet of pearls . . . One of the children put out her hand to get hold of the grand lady's spangles, but told her mother afterwards that she felt nothing.

This magnificent vision came on a prosaic errand; she wanted to borrow a bowl of oatmeal. In the Celtic legend of St Collen and the Fairy King, blue is introduced with red; the king's pages wear liveries of scarlet and blue, impolitely denounced by the saint as, 'Blue for the eternal cold and red for the flames of hell.' Manx fairies sometimes wore blue. In Gill's *Second Manx Scrapbook* (p. 248) we are told of a little gnomish man seen between Ramsey and Milntown, about two feet high,

wearing a red cap and a long blue coat with bright buttons, white hair and bushy whiskers. Face very wrinkled. Very bright, very kind eyes, carrying a small but very bright lantern.

In Jenkinson's *Guide to the Isle of Man, 1876* (p. 75) he reports being told by a farmer's wife that her mother always maintained that she had actually seen the fairies, and described them as young girls with 'scaly, fish-like hands and blue dresses'. The little mouse-sized fairies in the Suffolk story of Brother Mike wore blue coats, yellow breeches and little red caps. The fairies described by a friend to Walter Gill as seen in Glen Aldyn were greyish all over, something the colour of a fungus, a foot to eighteen inches high. The earth-bound trow in Shetland was also grey. A sombre note is struck too in Hugh Miller's account in *The Old Red Sandstone* of the departure of the fairies: the horses 'shaggy diminutive things, speckled dun and grey, the riders stunted, misgrown, ugly creatures, attired in antique jerkins of plaid, long grey cloaks, and little red caps, from which their wild, uncombed locks shot out over their cheeks and foreheads'. This confirms Kirk's much earlier statement that the fairies wore the costume of their country, as tartan in the Highlands.

John Beaumont's fairies, whose visits to him he describes in *A Treatise of Spirits* (1705), were dressed in a most unusual fashion:

They had both black, loose Network Gowns, tied with a black sash about their Middles, and within the Network appear'd a Gown of a Golden Colour, with somewhat of a Light striking through it; their Heads were not dressed with Topknots, but they had white Linnen Caps on, with lace about three Fingers breadth, and over it they had a Black loose Network Hood.

A rather engaging dress on little people of three feet high, but not at all the kind of costume one would expect to see on a fairy.

There were other eccentric costumes. The Gunna, a Highland fairy boy who had been banished from the court, wore fox skins; the kind, solitary Ghillie Dhu dressed in leaves and green moss; the sinister Northumbrian duergar wore a coat made of lambskin, trousers and shoes of moleskins and a hat of green moss decorated with a pheasant's feather. The Brown Man of the Muirs wore clothes of withered bracken. In the more literary descriptions of fairies from the sixteenth century onwards, they are said to wear clothes made of flowers, of gossamer spangled with dew and of silvery gauze, but these clothes are not so often found in the traditional accounts, though we can quote the foxglove caps of the shefro. Beyond these there are a number of fairies of all kinds who were naked. The asrai, the water-spirits, were beautiful, slender and naked, only covered by their long hair. Many of the nymph-like fairies danced naked in their rounds, as the witches were said to do, a fashion imitated by the modern witches. Many of the hobgoblins were naked. Brownies generally wore ragged clothes, but other hobgoblins were often hairy and naked. The Fenoderee is one of these hairy monsters. There is Lob-Lie-by-the-Fire, hob, or hobthrust, the bogan, and the uruisg who was like a satyr in shape. The Shetland broonie 'King of the Trows' was presumably naked, since he was laid by a gift of clothing. One naked little hobgoblin, however, was not shaggy, if we may trust his own pathetic description of himself:

> 'Little pixie, fair and slim,
> Not a rag to cover him.'

It is no wonder that that lament called forth the gift of clothing that laid him, but he did not go weeping away like the grogach of Man, but ran away merrily, as Mrs Bray tells us, chanting:

> 'Pixy fine, Pixy gay!
> Pixy now will run away.'

Some fairies wore clothes indistinguishable from those of mortals, fine and fashionable like those of Cherry's Master in the tale Cherry of Zennor, or homely and old-fashioned; or sometimes archaic, like the costume of the market people seen at the fairy market at Blackdown:

Those that had occasion to travel that way, have frequently seen them there, appearing like Men and Women of a stature generally near the smaller size of Men; their habits used to be of red, blew or green, according to the old way of Country Garb, with high crown'd hats.

Fairy Animals

The very numerous fairy animals, of which there are many traditions in the British Isles, may be divided into two main classes. There are wild ones, that exist for their own purposes and in their own right, and the domesticated ones bred and used by the fairies. It is sometimes difficult to distinguish between these two types, because the fairies occasionally allow their creatures to roam freely, as, for instance, the cu sith of the Highlands, which is generally kept as a watch dog in the brughs, but is at times free to roam at its pleasure, and the crodh mara, which sometimes visit human herds. But the distinction is generally clear.

The two kinds of fairy creatures occur very early in our traditions and are mentioned in the medieval chronicles. Examples are the grant, a medieval bogey-beast mentioned by Gervase of Tilbury, and the small dogs and horses to be found in Giraldus Cambrensis' story of Elidor.

Examples of the free fairy horses are the dangerous each uisge of the Highlands, the hardly less dangerous kelpies, the cabyll ushtey of the Isle of Man, and such bogies as the brag, the trash and the shock. All these have some power of shape-shifting. The horses used by the fairies occur everywhere in the heroic fairy legends, wherever there is the fairy rade in which they are to be found. They have been taken over by the Devil where he haunts with the yeth hounds or the devil's dandy dogs, and even with the cwn annwn, which once explicitly belonged to Gwyn ap Nudd. The fairy horses of the Tuatha de Danann are the most explicitly remembered.

The black dogs are the most common of the wild dogs in England, but there are many bogey-beast dogs, the barguest, the Gally-trot, the Mauthe Doog of Man, and the shock. The domestic fairy dogs most vividly remembered are Bran and Sceolan, the hunting dogs of Finn, and in the Cu Sith; but traditions of the hounds of the hills still linger in Somerset.

The fairy cattle were less fierce than the wild fairy horses. Occasionally these were independent, like the Dun Cow of Kirkham, and they were beneficent, not dangerous. The elf-bull was a lucky visitor to any herd, and so were the gwartheg y llyn of Wales. There were, however, ferocious ghost bulls like the Roaring Bull of Bagbury.

Of miscellaneous creatures, the most famous were the seal people, the selkies and roane. Cats were almost fairies in themselves, but there was a fairy cat in the Highlands, the cait sith, and a demon-god cat, Big Ears, which appeared after horrible invocations.

Afanc was a river monster of Wales, something like a giant beaver, and the Boobrie was a monstrous water-bird.

Goats and deer may be said to have been fairies in their own proper shape, and many birds, particularly the eagle, the raven, the owl and the wren, had strong fairy associations. Certain trout and salmon were fairy creatures, and even insects had their part: the Gooseberry Wife appeared as a gigantic hairy caterpillar. In fact the whole of these islands is rich in fairy zoology.

Changelings

The eagerness of fairies to possess themselves of human children is one of the oldest parts of the fairy beliefs and is a specific form of fairy theft. Mentions of the thefts of babies are to be found in the Medieval Chronicles of Ralph of Coggeshall and Gervase of Tilbury among others, through the Elizabethan and Jacobean times, and right down to the beginning of the present century. The fairies' normal method was to steal an unchristened child, who had not been given proper protection, out of the cradle and to leave a substitute in its place. This 'changeling' was of various kinds. Sometimes it was a stock of wood roughly shaped into the likeness of a child and endowed by glamour with a temporary appearance of life, which soon faded, when the baby would appear to die and the stock would be duly buried. More often a fairy child who did not thrive would be left behind, while the coveted, beautiful human baby was taken. More often still the changeling would be an ancient, withered fairy, of no more use to the fairy tribe and willing to lead an easy life being cherished, fed and carried about by its anxious foster-mother, wawling and crying for food and attention in an apparent state of paralysis.

The 'stock' method was most usually employed when the fairies had designs against the mother as well as the child. A good example of a frustrated attempt at such a theft is the Shetland tale 'Mind [Remember] da Crooked Finger'. The wife of a Shetland crofter had just given birth to her first child, and as her husband was folding his lambs he heard three loud knocks coming from underground. He closed the folds and walked by through the cornyard. As he came through the stacks he heard a loud voice say three times, 'Mind da crooked finger.' His wife had a crooked finger and he had a shrewd notion that the grey neighbours were planning an attack on his wife and his little bairn. But the good man knew what to do. He went quickly to the house, lighted a candle, took down a clasp-knife and a bible and opened them. As he did so a great clamour and wailing broke out in the byre, which was built against the house. He stuck the knife in his mouth with the blade pointing forward, held the lighted candle in one hand and the opened bible in the other, and made for the byre, followed by most of the neighbours who were visiting his wife. He opened the byre door and threw the bible inside, and as he did so the wailing redoubled, and with a great rush the fairies sped past him. They left behind them a wooden stock, carved feature by feature and joint by joint in the form of his wife. He lifted it up and carried it into the house. 'I've won this from the grey neighbours,' he said, 'and I'll make it serve my turn.' And for years afterwards he used the image as a chopping-block, and the wife was never molested by the fairies again.

A touching story of the weakling fairy child is told by Lady Wilde in *The Ancient Legends of Ireland*. This was of a very daring raid against a newly-born child. The mother and father were lying asleep when the door burst open and a tall, dark man came into the house, followed by an old hag with a wizened, hairy child in her arms. The mother roused her husband, who put up a vigorous resistance. His candle was twice blown out, but he seized the tongs, and forced the old hag out of the house. They re-lit the candle, and then they saw that their own baby was gone, and the hairy changeling was in its place. They burst into lamentations, but the door opened and a young girl wearing a red handkerchief came in. She asked them why they were crying, and when they showed her the changeling she laughed with joy and said, 'This is my own child that was stolen from me tonight because my people wanted to take your beautiful baby, but I'd rather have ours; if you let me take him I will tell you how to get your child back.' They gave the changeling to her with joy, and she told them to take three sheaves to the fairy hill, and to burn them one by one, threatening to burn everything that grew on the hill if the fairies did not return their baby safe and sound. They did so, and got their own child back again. The threat to burn the thorns on the fairy hill is sometimes employed to win back full-grown humans.

When the changeling is supposed, like this one, to be a fairy child it is often tormented or exposed to induce the fairy parents to change it back again. This method has been responsible for a dreadful amount of child suffering, particularly in Ireland. Even at the beginning of this century a child was burned to death by officious neighbours who put it on a red-hot shovel in the expectation that it would fly up the chimney. Waldron in his *Isle of Man* gives a tragic account of a dumb child who was supposed to be a changeling. Infantile paralysis or any other unfamiliar disease among the various blights and illnesses that came on suddenly would be accounted for by supposing that the child had been changed, and as a rule the parents would be advised to beat it, expose it on a fairy hill or throw it on to the fire. Only occasionally were they advised to treat the child kindly so that their own children might be kindly treated in return.

Where the changeling was an old fairy it was thought possible to trick it into betraying its age. The method used was so common that it is surprising that the fairies were not forewarned of it. It was to take some two dozen empty eggshells, set them carefully up on the hearth and go through the motions of brewing. Then the constant sobbing and whining would gradually cease, the supine form would raise itself, and in a shrill voice the thing would cry 'I have seen the first acorn before the oak, but I have never seen brewing done in eggshells before!' Then it only remained to stoke up the fire and throw the changeling on to it, when he would fly up the chimney, laughing and shrieking, and the true baby would come to the door. Sometimes the child would not be returned and the parents would have to go and rescue it from the fairy hill.

Children were supposed to be stolen into Fairyland either to pay a teind to the Devil, to reinforce the fairy stock or for love of their beauty. Where older people were stolen it was for specific qualities and they were replaced by some form of the 'stock' and generally seemed to be suffering from a 'stroke', which is indeed 'the fairy stroke', generally given by elf-shot. The true changelings are those fairy creatures that replace the stolen human babies.

The Fairy Market

The most famous of the fairy markets was held in Somerset at Blackdown near Pitminster. It is first mentioned in detail by Bovet in his *Pandaemonium, or The Devil's Cloyster* (p. 207). It is quoted by Keightley:

At some times they would seem to dance, at other times to keep a great fair or market. I made it my business to enquire among the neighbours what credit might be given to that which was reported of them, and by many of the neighbouring inhabitants I had this account confirmed.

The place near which they most ordinarily showed themselves was on the side of a hill, named Black-down, between the parishes of Pittminster and Chestonford, not many miles from Taunton. Those that have had occasion to travel that way have frequently seen them, appearing like men and women, of a stature generally near the smaller size of men. Their habits used to be of red, blue or green, according to the old way of country garb, with high crowned hats. One time about fifty years since, a person living at Comb St Nicholas, a parish lying on one side of that hill, near Chard, was riding towards his home that way, and saw, just before him, on that side of the hill, a great company of people, that seemed to him like country folks assembled at a fair. There were all sorts of commodities, to his appearance, as at our ordinary fairs; pewterers, shoemakers, pedlars, with all kinds of trinkets, fruit and drinking booths. He could not remember anything which he had usually seen at fairs but what he saw there. It was once in his thoughts that it might be some fair for Chestonford, there being a considerable one at some time of the year; but then again he considered that it was not the season for it. He was under very great surprise, and admired what the meaning of what he saw should be. At length it came to his mind what he had heard concerning the Fairies on the side of that hill, and it being near the road he was to take, he resolved to ride in amongst them, and see what they were. Accordingly he put on his horse that way, and, though he saw them perfectly all along as he came, yet when he was upon the place where all this had appeared to him, he could discern nothing at all, only seemed to be crowded and thrust, as when one passes through a throng of people. All the rest became invisible to him until he came to a little distance, and then it appeared to him again as at first. He found himself in pain, and so hastened home; where, being arrived, lameness seized him all on one side, which continued on him as long as he lived, which was many years; for he was living in Comb, and gave an account to any that enquired of this accident for more than twenty years afterwards; and this relation I had from a person of known honour, who had it from the man himself.

There were some whose names I have now forgot, but they then lived at a gentleman's house, named Comb Farm, near the place before specified; both the man, his wife, and divers of the neighbours, assured me they had, at many times, seen this *fair-keeping* in the summer-time, as they came from Taunton-market, but they durst not adventure in amongst them; for that everyone that had done so had received great damage by it.

These fairies evidently felt the common fairy dislike of human prying and infringements of fairy privacy, and an even more sinister fair, merry and beautiful as it appeared at first sight, is to be found in Lady Wilde's *Ancient Legends of Ireland*, 'November Eve' (vol. I, p. 145), in which the fairies are described as fairies and yet are identified with the dead.

The fairies of Blackdown, however, seem to have had their gentler moods. Ruth Tongue in *County Folk-Lore* (vol. VIII, p. 112) says that the pixies have now taken over Somerset from the fairies and hold their fair in the same place. She tells of a covetous old fellow who saw the pixy fair and took a fancy to a gold mug there. He urged his pony into the middle of the fair, seized the mug and made off. In the morning, when he went to look at his prize, it had turned into a great toadstool, and the pony was scamble-footed, or lame, for the rest of his days.

In a rather earlier story, pieced together in Miss Tongue's youth, pixies are called 'vairies' and receive an old friend courteously, rewarding his good manners by turning an apparent payment of withered leaves into gold, reversing the more usual procedure.

There were a Varmer over-right our place did zee the vairies to their Market, and comed whoame zafe tew. Mind, he did'n never vorget to leave hearth clean 'n a pail of well water vor'n at night, 'n a girt dish of scalt cream tew. My granny did zay her'd get'n ready vor'n many's the time. Zo when her rode up tew stall, zee, all among the Vair, 'n axed mannerly vor a zider-mug a-hanging up, the vairies answers 'n zo purty as if they were to Taunton Market. With that Varmer lugs out his money-bag 'n pays, 'n what do 'ee believe! They gived 'n a heap of dead leaves vor his change, quite serious like, Varmer he took 'n serious tew, then her wishes 'n 'Good-night, arl,' 'n her ride whoame. He d' put zider mug on table, 'n spread they dead leaves round 'n careful, then he d' zay, 'Come morn, they won't none o' they be yur, but 'twere worth it to zee the liddle dears' Market.'

Come morn, when Varmer went to get his dew-bit avore ploughing what do 'ee zee on table but a vine silver mug 'n lumps of gold all round 'n.

Here we have the fairies at their most benign; Christina Rossetti's goblin market shows them at their most sinister.

It is true enough to some fairy traditions, but it is possible that she evolved it out of her own imagination. It was not, at any rate, the fairies' own market, but a travelling show designed to beguile and entrap mortals.

Fairy Trees

Nearly all trees have some sacred association from very early times, but some are more sacred than others. There is the magical trilogy of oak and ash and thorn. There are the fruit-bearing trees, especially apple and hazel; there are rowan, holly and willow, elder and alder. Some trees seem to be regarded as having a personality of their own, and some are more specifically a haunt of fairies or spirits. Most people would probably think first of an oak as a sacred tree, worshipped by the Druids, and it is strong enough certainly to stand in its own right, though everyone knows the couplet,

Fairy folks
Are in old oaks,

and many oak coppices are said to be haunted by the sinister oakmen. Hawthorn has certain qualities of its own, but it is primarily thought of as a tree sacred to or haunted by the fairies. This is especially so of solitary thorns growing near fairy hills, or of a ring of three or more hawthorns. White may in blossom was supposed to bring death into the house, and although it was brought round on May Morning it was hung up outside.

Ruth Tongue collected a folk-song in Somerset whose chorus illustrates the popular belief about three very different trees:

> Ellum do grieve,
> Oak he do hate,
> Willow do walk
> If you travels late.

Possibly because of the vulnerability of elms to disease, it was thought that if one elm was cut down a neighbouring elm would pine and die in sympathy. Oaks, however, as fitted their ancient, god-like status, bitterly resented being cut, and an oak coppice which sprang from the roots of a felled oakwood was malevolent and dangerous to travel through by night, more especially if it was a bluebell wood. Willows were even more sinister, for they had a habit of uprooting themselves on a dark night and following a solitary traveller, muttering. Tolkien is faithful to folk tradition in the ogre-ish behaviour of Old Man Willow. Wood-Martin, in his *Traces of the Elder Faiths of Ireland*, devotes some attention to tree beliefs. For instance, speaking of the sacred ash, he mentions one in the parish of Clenor in County Cork, whose branches were never cut, though firewood was scarce all round, and another in Borrisokane, the old Bell Tree, sacred to May Day rites, of which it was believed that if any man burnt even a chip of it on his hearth his whole house would be burned down. A similar fate was brought down on himself by a cottager who tried to cut a branch from a sacred elder overhanging a saint's well. He tried three times; twice he stopped because his house seemed to be on fire, but found it a false alarm. The third time he determined not to be put off by appearances and carried the branch home, only to find his cottage burnt to the ground. He had had his warning. There are two views of the elder. It has been a sacred tree, as we may see from Hans Andersen's 'Elder-Flower Mother'. In Lincolnshire, too, it used to be thought necessary to ask the tree's permission before cutting a branch. The formula was 'Owd Gal, give me of thy wood, an Oi will give some of moine, when I graws inter a tree' (*County Folk-Lore*, vol. v, p. 21). The flowers and fruit were much esteemed for wine, the tree was a shelter against flies, and it was said also that the good fairies found protection under it from witches and evil spirits. On the other hand, in Oxfordshire and the Midlands, many elders were strongly suspected of being transformed witches, and they were supposed to bleed if they were cut. The witch of the Rollright Stones took the form of an elder tree according to the popular legend. D. A. Mac Manus in *The Middle Kingdom*, an explanation of comparatively modern fairy beliefs in Ireland, devotes a chapter to fairy trees, and gives many examples of the judgements falling on people who have destroyed sacred thorn trees. He believes some trees to be haunted by fairies and others by demons, and gives one example of a close group of three trees, two thorns and an elder, which was haunted by three evil spirits. He says that when an oak and ash and thorn grew close together, a twig taken from each, bound with red thread, was thought to be a protection against spirits of the night.

In England, ash was a protection against mischievous spirits, but in Scotland the mountain ash, rowan, was even more potent, probably because of its red berries:

> Rowan, lammer (amber) and red threid
> Pits witches to their speed,

as the old saying went. Red was always a vital and conquering colour. A berried holly was potent for good. On the other hand, a barren one – that is, one that bore only male flowers – was thought to be malevolent and dangerous. Two fruit-bearing trees, apple and hazel, had specially magical qualities. Hazel-nuts were the source of wisdom and also of fertility, and apples of power and youth. There was some danger attached to each of them. An 'ymp-tree' – that is, a grafted apple – was under fairy influence, and a man who slept under it was liable, as Sir Lancelot found, to be carried away by fairy ladies. A somewhat similar fate befell Queen Meroudys in the medieval poem of King Orfeo. The fertility powers of nut-trees could be overdone, and the Devil was said to be abroad in the woods at the time of nut-gathering; 'so many cratches, so many cradles', goes the Somerset saying quoted by Ruth Tongue in *County Folk-Lore* (vol. VIII). On the other hand, the hazel-nuts eaten by trout or salmon gave their flesh a power of imparting wisdom at the first taste of it. It was to this that Finn owed his tooth of wisdom.

Mac Manus mentions other fairy trees, Scots fir, birch, blackthorn and broom, though this last is a shrub rather than a tree. A beech is a holy tree, with no connection with fairies. It is said that the prayers spoken under it go straight to Heaven. Otherwise it is difficult to think of a tree which has not some fairy connection.

Fashions in Fairy-Lore

Even the most flaccid and degenerate of the literary fairies have some point in common with the fairies in folk tradition, but, as a rule, the poets and story-tellers pick out one aspect from the varied and intricate world of fairy tradition, and the aspect chosen differs not only from poet to poet but from one period to another. The fairies of medieval romances are among the heroic fairies in type, of human size and often amorous of mortals, expert in enchantment and glamour, generally beautiful but occasionally hideous hags. Many of them are half-forgotten gods and goddesses, euhemerized into mortals with magical powers. The goddesses are more frequent than the gods. It was literary fashion which chose out this type because the romances derived from Celtic hero tales founded on the Celtic Pantheon; scattered references in the medieval chronicles show that very different types of fairies were available to the medieval poets if they had chosen to use them.

A different type of spirit, though no less true to tradition, appears among the Elizabethan and Jacobean fairies. It is true that Spenser uses the fairies, enchanters and witches of the Arthurian legends in the machinery of his Faerie Queene, but on the whole the spotlight is turned upon the diminutive fairies. They appear in John Lyly's *Endimion*, in the anonymous *Maides Metamorphosis* and the *Wisdome of Dr Dodypol*, and above all in *A Midsummer Night's Dream*. Queen Mab in *Romeo and Juliet* is even more minute than the elves who waited on Titania. The Jacobean poets followed hard on the fashion. The diminutive fairies in Drayton, Herrick, *et al.*, made an extravaganza of Shakespeare's little fairies until, with the Duchess of Newcastle, they became miracles of littleness. Even Milton in *Paradise Lost* used the elves to illustrate diminution and small size. The exception to these dainty and miniature fairies is the rougher, homely hobgoblin, by whatever name he is called – Robin Goodfellow, Puck or the Lubbard Fiend. Since that period, the tiny fairies have constantly haunted literature.

The eighteenth century was the first period in which books were written expressly for the edification of children. Educational text books had been written before – one of the first books printed was Caxton's *Babees Book* to train pages in etiquette, and there were Latin and French conversation books, but works of fiction were first written expressly for children in the eighteenth century. At the end of the seventeenth century the sophisticated French fairy-stories of Perrault and Madame D'Aulnoy were translated into English. They began as real traditional tales, polished to meet the taste of the French court, and they were equally popular in England. Half the court seem to have tried their hands at them, and as time went on they moved farther away from their original. The fairy godmothers, already at one remove from folk fairies, became relentless moralists, driving their protégés along the path to virtue. The trend persisted into the nineteenth century, and it was not until a quarter of it had passed that the researches of the folklorists began to have some effect on children's literature. The Romantic Revival, however, had begun before this to affect the writings of the poets. Collins, Scott, Hogg and Keats wrote in the folk-fairy tradition, and as the century went on writers of children's stories followed them; Jean Ingelow and J. H. Ewing are among the best. At the beginning of the twentieth century, an extreme tenderness and sensibility about children almost overwhelmed the folk fairies and turned them into airy, tenuous, pretty creatures without meat or muscles, made up of froth and whimsy. Rudyard

Kipling fought against this tendency in *Puck of Pook's Hill*, and now, in Tolkien, his predecessors and successors, we enjoy a world in which imagination has superseded fancy; but whimsy is still with us in the works of the weaker writers.

Infringement of Fairy Privacy

From the earliest times the fairies have been noted as secret people. They do not like to be watched, their land must not be trespassed on, their kindnesses must not be boasted of. Fairy lovers come and go in secret. Dame Tryamour, the lover of Sir Launfal in the twelfth-century metrical romance, comes and goes invisible to mortal eyes, and her love must not be boasted of. When Launfal is goaded into talking of her, all the costly presents he has been given melt away and he is left to poverty. In the end, however, his fairy relents and takes him back to favour, an unusually happy ending to what is almost invariably a tragedy. In one of the Highland legends in *Waifs and Strays of Celtic Tradition* (vol. v), 'The Two Sisters and the Curse', Mairearad (Margaret) has a fairy lover who forbids her to speak of him, but in a moment of confidence she tells her sister about him, who promises that it will 'as soon pass from her knee as from her lips'. She is false to her word, however, and spreads the tale, so that Margaret loses her lover. She wanders away from home and into the hills where she is heard singing laments until at length she fades away. Nothing more is seen of her until she or her child comes out of the cairn to avenge Dun Ailsa's treachery on Brown Torquil, her son.

One of the commonest tales from Elizabethan times to the present day is of mortals favoured by the fairies, who have been given fairy money till they tell the source of it, when the gifts cease for ever. This trait is often mentioned in Elizabethan accounts of the fairies, and exactly the same story is recorded in the archives of the School of Scottish Studies, and a similar anecdote, 'Fairy Money', is told also by Seán O' Súilleabháin in *Folktales of Ireland*. Fairy privacy must be respected even by passers-by. The girl who saw Wild Edric's Rade was told by her father to put an apron over her head so as not to watch them. In Bowker's *Goblin Tales of Lancashire*, the two villagers who see the fairy funeral pass by withdraw beneath an oak to avoid being seen, and only when their curiosity is excited do they press forward to see the corpse on the bier and recognize it as the younger of the pair. In many Irish anecdotes, people sleeping innocently on a fairy hill have been blinded or pushed over a rock by the angry fairies who inhabit it. In Ulster, people avoid fairy roads, especially on quarter days, when the fairies are ordinarily on the move.

In short, though fairies are ready to reveal themselves to mortals whom they favour, or whose services they wish to secure, they are quick to resent and revenge any presumption upon that favour.

Thefts from Fairies

It would perhaps not be quite fair to say that men stole as much from the fairies as the fairies stole from men by way of fairy thefts, but, considering the awe in which the fairies were held, it is surprising how many attempts, some of them successful, were made to take gold or silver plate out of the fairy mounds. The first accounts are in the Medieval Chronicles. There is the story of Elidor and his attempted theft of the golden ball which belonged to the little fairy prince, in order to satisfy his mother's curiosity. William of Newbridge tells of a barrow near his birthplace in Yorkshire which was occasionally open, with lights streaming from it and feasting going on inside. One night a peasant passed it and was invited in and offered a cup of wine. He poured out the contents and carried off the cup, which was afterwards given to Henry I. Gervase of Tilbury tells what seems like a variant of this fairy cup story, though told of a different place. It is of a fairy cup-bearer who appeared from a mound near Gloucester and offered drink to any huntsman who asked for it. One was so ungrateful as to carry off the cup and present it to the Earl of Gloucester, who, however, executed him as a robber and gave the cup to Henry I. The Luck of Edenhall was stolen by the butler of Edenhall from a fairy gathering in something the same way, and carried with it a curse. Later attempts, like that of the miser on the fairy gump, have often ended in ignominious failure. Ruth Tongue in *County Folk-Lore* (vol. VIII) tells the story of a farmer who saw the fairy market on Blackdown and tried to snatch a gold mug off one of the stalls. He galloped off with it, got safe home and took the mug to bed with him. Next morning there was nothing there but a large toadstool, and when he went down to look at his pony it was 'scamble-footed' and remained so for the rest of its life. J. G. Campbell in his *Superstitions of the Highlands and Islands of Scotland* (pp. 52–7) gives several variants of the story of Luran, in some of which the hero is a dog, and in some a human – a crofter or a boy butler. In one version the fairies steal from Luran and he tries to make up his losses by stealing from the fairies. He is not finally successful. A feature of the story is the friendly adviser among the fairies. He is generally called 'The Red-headed Man' and is supposed to be a captured human who retains his sympathy with his fellow men:

The Charmed Hill (*Beinn Shianta*), from its height, greenness, or pointed summit, forms a conspicuous object on the Ardnamurchan coast, at the north entrance of the Sound of Mull. On 'the shoulder' of this hill, were two hamlets, Sginid and Corryvulin, the lands attached to which, now forming part of a large sheep farm, were at one time occupied in common by three tenants, one of whom was named Luran Black (*Luran Mac-ille-dhui*). One particular season a cow of Luran's was found unaccountably dead each morning. Suspicion fell on the tenants of the Culver (*an cuilibheir*), a green knoll in Corryvulin, having the reputation of being tenanted by the Fairies. Luran resolved to watch his cattle for a night, and ascertain the cause of his mysterious losses. Before long he saw the Culver opening, and a host of little people pouring out. They surrounded a grey cow (*mart glas*) belonging to him and drove it into the knoll. Not one busied himself in doing this more than Luran himself; he was, according to the Gaelic expression, 'as one and as two' (*mar a h-aon's mar a dhà*) in his exertions. The cow was killed and skinned. An old Elf, a tailor sitting in the upper part of the brugh, with a needle in the right lappel of his coat, was forcibly caught hold of, stuffed into the cow's hide, and sewn up. He was then taken to the door and rolled down the slope. Festivities commenced, and whoever might be on the floor dancing, Luran was sure to be. He was 'as one and as two' at the dance, as he had been at driving the cow. A number of gorgeous cups and dishes were put on the table, and Luran, resolving to make up

43

for the loss of the grey cow, watched his opportunity and made off with one of the cups (*còrn*). The Fairies observed him and started in pursuit. He heard one of them remark:

> 'Not swift would be Luran
> If it were not the hardness of his bread.'

His pursuers were likely to overtake him, when a friendly voice called out:

> 'Luran, Luran Black,
> Betake thee to the black stones of the shore.'

Below high water marks, no Fairy, ghost, or demon can come, and, acting on the friendly advice, Luran reached the shore, and keeping below the tide mark made his way home in safety. He heard the outcries of the person who had called out to him (probably a former acquaintance who had been taken by 'the people') being belaboured by the Fairies for his ill-timed officiousness. Next morning, the grey cow was found lying dead with its feet in the air, at the foot of the Culver, and Luran said that a needle would be found in its right shoulder. On this proving to be the case, he allowed none of the flesh to be eaten, and threw it out of the house.

One of the fields, tilled in common by Luran and two neighbours, was every year, when ripe, reaped by the Fairies in one night, and the benefit of the crop disappeared. An old man was consulted, and he undertook to watch the crop. He saw the shïan of Corryvulin open, and a troop of people coming out. There was an old man at their head, who put the company in order, some to shear, some to bind the sheaves, and some to make stooks. On the word of command being given, the field was reaped in a wonderfully short time. The watcher, calling aloud, counted the reapers. The Fairies never troubled the field again.

Their persecution of Luran did not, however, cease. While on his way to Inveraray Castle, with his Fairy cup, he was lifted mysteriously with his treasure out of the boat, in which he was taking his passage, and was never seen or heard of after.

Protection Against Fairies

People walking alone by night, especially through fairy-haunted places, had many ways of protecting themselves. The first might be by sacred symbols, by making the sign of the cross or by carrying a cross, particularly one made of iron; by prayers or the chanting of hymns, by holy water, sprinkled or carried, and by carrying and strewing churchyard mould in their path. Bread and salt were also effective, and both were regarded as sacred symbols, one of life and the other of eternity. As Herrick says:

> For that holy piece of bread
> Charmes the danger and the dread.

Bells were protective; church bells, the bells worn by morris dancers and the bells round the necks of sheep and oxen. So was whistling and the snapping of clappers. A man who was pixy-led, wandering around and unable to find his way out of the field, would generally turn his coat. This act of turning clothes may have been thought to act as a change of identity, for gamblers often turned their coat to break a run of bad luck.

Certain plants and herbs were also protective counter-charms. The strongest was a four-leafed clover, which broke fairy glamour, as well as the fairy ointment, which was indeed said by Hunt to be made of four-leafed clovers. St John's wort, the herb of Midsummer, was potent against spells and the power of fairies, evil spirits and the Devil. Red verbena was almost equally potent, partly perhaps because of its pure and brilliant colour. Daisies, particularly the little field daisies, were protective plants, and a child wearing daisy chains was supposed to be safe from fairy kidnapping. Red-berried trees were also protective, above them all rowan or mountain ash. A staff made of rowan wood or a rowan cross or a bunch of ripe berries were all sure protections, and where rowan did not grow ash was a good substitute.

If chased by evil fairies, one could generally leap to safety across running water, particularly a southward-flowing stream, though there were evil water spirits such as the kelpie who haunted fresh-water streams.

A newly-christened child was safe against being carried off by the fairies, but before christening 'the little pagan' was kept safe by his father's trousers laid over the cradle, or an open pair of scissors hung above it. This last had a double potency as being made of steel and as hanging in the form of a cross, on the same principle that the child's garments were secured by pins stuck in cross-wise. The house and stock were protected by iron horseshoes above the house and stable doors, and horses were protected from being elf-ridden by self-bored stones hung above the manger.

With so many methods of protection, it was surprising that such a number of babies were stolen and replaced by changelings and so many travellers were pixy-led.

Differing Ideas on Fairy Origin

The people who believed in their existence had differing notions about the origin of fairies. Folklorists are more concerned in the origin of fairy beliefs; what is important to them is not so much whether the fairies really exist as whether their existence is actually believed in by the people who tell about them. When that has been discovered, the folklorist's next object is to find out the grounds on which the belief was founded. Various suggestions have been put forward, either as full or partial solutions of the problem.

One of the most well-supported is that which equates the fairies with the dead. Lewis Spence in *British Fairy Origins* makes a very plausible case for this theory. He can bring forward plenty of evidence from tradition, as, for instance, Lady Wilde's accounts of Finvarra's court, and Bottrell's story 'The Fairy Dwelling on Selena Moor'. According to Kirk, the fairy knowes by the churchyard were supposed to be places where the souls of the dead lodged, waiting to rejoin their bodies on the Day of

Judgement. The small size of the fairies might be plausibly accounted for by the primitive idea of the soul as a miniature replica of the man himself, which emerged from the owner's mouth in sleep or unconsciousness. If its return was prevented, the man died.

David Mac Ritchie in *The Testimony of Tradition* and other writings was the chief exponent of the theory that the fairy beliefs were founded on the memory of a more primitive race driven into hiding by the invaders, lurking in caves or fens, some of them half-domesticated and doing chores about the houses like the shaggy and unkempt brownie. Such tales as 'The Isle of Sanntraigh' give verisimilitude to the theory, but it does not cover all forms of fairy belief.

A third suggestion which attempts to cover only part of the ground is that the fairies are dwindled gods or nature spirits. This was undoubtedly true of the daoine sidh and possibly of the tylwyth teg, and of a few of the more primitive spirits such as the Cailleach Bheur, the Hag of Winter, Black Annis and so on. Tree and water spirits might also be traced to this source. The psychological foundation of folk-tales, explored at some depth by C. G. Jung, may afford some valuable hints to folklorists probing into the foundation of fairy beliefs, and their curious plausibility as if the mind leapt to receive them. On the whole we may say that it is unwise to commit oneself blindfold to any solitary theory of the origins of fairy belief, but that it is most probable that these are all strands in a tightly twisted cord.

Time in Fairyland

The early fairy specialists had a vivid sense of the relativity of time, founded, perhaps, on experiences of dream or trance, when a dream that covers several years may be experienced between rolling out of bed and landing on the floor. Occasionally the dimension is in this direction. Hartland, in his exhaustive study of 'The Supernatural Lapse of Time in Fairyland', contained in *The Science of Fairy Tales*, gives a Pembrokeshire example of a visit to Fairyland (p. 199). A young shepherd joined a fairy dance and found himself in a glittering palace surrounded by most beautiful gardens, where he passed many years in happiness among the fairy people. There was only one prohibition: in the middle of the garden there was a fountain, filled with gold and silver fish, and he was told he must on no account drink out of it. He desired increasingly to do so, and at last he plunged his hands into the pool. At once the whole place vanished, and he found himself on the cold hillside among his sheep. Only minutes had passed since he joined the fairy dance. More often this trance-like experience is told in a more theological setting, the journey of Mahomet to Paradise, for instance, or the experience of Brahmins or hermits. As a rule, however, time moves in the other direction, both in visits to Fairyland and to other supernatural worlds. A dance of a few minutes takes a year and a day of common time, as, in the tale of 'Rhys and Llewellyn', a few days of feasting and merriment have consumed 200 years in the mortal world (see King Herla). This is not always so, for nothing in folk tradition can be contained in an exact and logical system. Elidurus could go backwards and forwards between Fairyland and his home with no alteration of time, human midwives to the fairies can visit fairy homes and return the same night, the man who borrowed fairy ointment from the fairy hill was taken into it with impunity, and Isobel Gowdie visited the fairy hills in the same way to obtain elf-shot. Yet, on the whole, it may be said that the man who visits Fairyland does so at a grave risk of not returning until long after his span of mortal life has been consumed.

Sometimes, as in the Rip Van Winkle tale, a broken taboo, the partaking of fairy food or drink in Fairyland, is followed by an enchanted sleep during which time passes at a supernatural rate, but it is not always so.

Certainly King Herla and his companions feasted in Fairyland, but there seems no suggestion that the passage of time was caused by this communion. The effect of the visit was disastrous, but the intention does not seem to have been unfriendly.

The Ossian story, in which the hero goes to live with a fairy bride and returns after some hundreds of years, is widespread and is even to be found among the best-known of the Japanese fairy-tales, 'Urashima Taro'. Here, as in many other versions, his bride is a sea-maiden. Fairyland is often under or across the sea, and mermaids are amorous of mortals. When Urashima tries to return home, his bride gives him a casket in which his years are locked, and old age and death come on him when he opens it. Hartland in *The Science of Fairy Tales* (p. 141) noted an interesting Italian variant of the Ossian tale. In this, which begins as a swan maiden tale, the hero's bride is Fortune, and after once losing her, he follows her to the Isle of Happiness, where he stays, as he thinks, for two months, but it is really 200 years. When he insists on returning to visit his mother, Fortune gives him a magnificent black horse to carry him over the sea, and warns him not to dismount from it, but she is more prudent than Niam of the Golden Locks, for she goes with him. They ride over the sea together, and find a changed country. As they go towards his mother's house they meet an old hag with a carriage-load of old shoes behind her, which she has worn out looking for him. She slips and falls to the ground, and he is bending down to lift her when Fortune calls out: 'Beware! That is Death!' So they ride on. Next they meet a great lord on a leg-weary horse, which founders at their side, but before the hero can come to his aid, Fortune cries out again: 'Be careful! That is the Devil!' And they ride on. But when the hero finds that his mother is dead and long since forgotten, he turns back with his bride to the Isle of Happiness, and has lived there with her ever since. This is one of the few stories of fairy brides and visits to Fairyland which ends happily.

One of the same motifs occurs in a Tyrolean story, also told by Hartland (p. 185). A peasant followed his herd under a stone and into a cave, where a lady met him, gave him food and offered him a post as a gardener. He worked in the country for some weeks, and then began to be homesick. They let him go home, but when he got back everything was strange, and no one recognized him except one old crone, who came up to him and said, 'Where have you been? I have been looking for you for 200 years.' She took him by the hand, and he fell dead, for she was Death.

When people return in this way after long absence they often fall to dust as soon as they eat human food. This is especially so in the Welsh stories. In a Highland version two men who had returned from Fairyland on a Sunday went to church, and as soon as the scriptures were read they crumbled into dust.

The suggestion behind all these stories is that Fairyland is a world of the dead, and that those who entered it had long been dead, and carried back with them an illusory body which crumbled into dust when they met reality.

In Ruth Tongue's moving story 'The Noontide Ghost' in *Forgotten Folk-Tales of the English Counties* (p. 53), this transformation has already occurred. The old man who long ago met the 'queer sort of chap' who delayed him with wagering-games and old merriment, returned as a ghost to look for his long-dead wife, and was called by her up to Heaven after he had told his story to a mortal listener. As in this tale, the fairy condition, or indeed the entry into eternity, often needs no entry into a geographical fairyland, underground or underwater. A fairy ring, the encounter with a fairy rade, the singing of a supernatural bird, is enough to surround the mortal with the supernatural condition, so that he stands invisible and rapt away from the mortal world which continues all around him until the mysterious time-pattern ceases to have potency. For it is to be noticed that, whatever the differences in pace, human time and fairy time somehow interlock. The dancer in the fairy circle is nearly always to be rescued after a year and a day, sometimes after an exact year; two months equal 200 years; an hour may be a day and a night; there is some relationship. And if times are somehow interconnected, seasons are even more important. May Day, Midsummer Eve, Hallowe'en are all times when the doors open between the worlds. James Stephens's *In the Land of Youth*, a translation of one of the early Irish fairy legends, is a good example of this. Certain times of day are important too. The four hinges of the day, noontide, dusk, midnight and early dawn, are cardinal to the fairies. Certain days of the week are also important, days of danger and days of escape. In fact, however free and wild the course of fairy time appears to be, we find here as elsewhere traces of the dependence of fairies upon mortals.

Elizabethan Fairies

The fairies of the medieval romances grew out of the Celtic tradition of the heroic fairies, the knights and ladies of the Mabinogion, the Daoine Sidh who encountered the Milesians in love or battle; but the poets and dramatists of the Elizabethan age brought a different strand of fairy tradition into prominence. This was partly because the rise of the yeoman class, as the 16th century went on, had brought a spread of literacy and produced a new class of writers, drawn from the country up to town as Shakespeare was drawn, and bringing with them their own country traditions. The fairy ladies of the romances had become more humanized and sophisticated as time went on, and though Spenser clung to them still, they were perhaps slightly out of date. Classical mythology was a perennial source of allusions familiar to every lettered man, even if he only came from a small-town grammar school. Still, there had been a good deal said and sung about Mars and Venus and naiads and dryads and nymphs; a new source of reference would be a welcome change, and it was at hand in the English countryside. There are two main types of fairies which were novelties in literature: the hobgoblins, with which we may rate the brownie and the puck, and the small, flower-loving fairies such as we find pre-eminently in *A Midsummer Night's Dream* and which became all the fashion for the Jacobean fairies. These fairy writings came in towards the end of the century, in the hey-day of the drama.

Among the prose writers, Nashe in his *Terrors of the Night* gives us a characteristic picture of the hobgoblin type:

The Robbin-good-fellowes, Elfes, Fairies, Hobgoblins of our latter age, which idolatrous former daies and the fantasticall world of Greece ycleaped *Fawnes, Satyres, Dryades*, & *Hama-dryades*, did most of their merry prankes in the Night. Then ground they malt, and had hempen shirts for their labours, daunst in rounds in greene meadowes, pincht maids in their sleep that swept not their houses cleane, and led poore Travellers out of their way notoriously.

Here Nashe, with a journalist's eye, lights on most of the things which became most noteworthy in his period, the brownie labours and the gift of a shirt that brought them to an end, the dancing in fairy rings, the love of order and neatness and the punishment for untidy ways and the misleading of night wanderers.

Shakespeare puts in all of these, except the pinching, which is being forever mentioned in the masques and poems, but he adds the fairy smallness and their love of flowers, which were to become so characteristic of the Jacobean fairies.

The Denham Tracts

The author of these, Michael Aislabie Denham, died in 1859, nearly thirty years before the Folk-Lore Society was founded. Nevertheless, he worked at the study of folklore for a great part of his life, and contributed to Hone's *Everyday Book* and Richardson's *Table Book*. *A Collection of Proverbs and Popular Sayings* was published for him by the Percy Society, and he printed quite a number of pamphlets and short books during the last years of his life. A great deal of this, however, was scattered and dispersed when he died, and when the Folk-Lore Society was first founded in 1878, W. J. Thoms suggested that Denham's papers should be collected and published. The result of this suggestion was the publication by the Folk-Lore Society of *The Denham Tracts* in two volumes (1892 and 1895). The first volume chiefly consists of local sayings and proverbs, but spirit and fairy traditions are to be found scattered about in the second, which contains much that is quotable. Of particular interest is the voluminous list (vol. II, pp. 77–80) of the fairies and other night fears which troubled our ancestors. One section of it is borrowed straight from the list given by Reginald Scot in his *Discovery of Witchcraft*, but a great deal of local lore has been added to this, and many of the spirits mentioned have received separate treatment in the present dictionary, though it requires rather a long stretch to include some among spirits:

Grose observes, too, that those born on Christmas Day cannot see spirits; which is another incontrovertible fact. What a happiness this must have been seventy or eighty years ago and upwards, to those chosen few who had the good luck to be born on the eve of this festival, of all festivals; when the whole earth was so overrun with ghosts, boggles, bloody-bones, spirits, demons, ignis fatui, brownies, bugbears, black dogs, spectres, shellycoats, scarecrows, witches, wizards, barguests, Robin-Goodfellows, hags, night-bats, scrags, breaknecks, fantasms, hobgoblins, hobhoulards, boggy-boes, dobbies, hobthrusts, fetches, kelpies, warlocks, mock-beggars, mum-pokers, Jemmy-burties, urchins, satyrs, pans, fauns, sirens, tritons, centaurs, calcars, nymphs, imps, incubusses, spoorns, men-in-the-oak, hell-wains, fire-drakes, kit-a-can-sticks, Tom-tumblers, melch-dicks, larrs, kitty-witches, hobby-lanthorns, Dick-a-Tuesdays, Elf-fires, Gylburnt-tails, knockers, elves, raw-heads, Meg-with-the-wads, old-shocks, ouphs, pad-foots, pixies, pictrees, giants, dwarfs, Tom-pokers, tutgots, snapdragons, sprets, spunks, conjurers, thurses, spurns, tantarrabobs, swaithes, tints, tod-lowries, Jack-in-the-Wads, mormos, changelings, redcaps, yeth-hounds, colt-pixies, Tom-thumbs, black-bugs, boggarts, scar-bugs, shag-foals, hodge-pochers, hob-thrushes, bugs, bull-beggars, bygorns, bolls, caddies, bomen, brags, wraithes, waffs, flay-boggarts, fiends, gallytrots, imps, gytrashes, patches, hob-and-lanthorns, gringes, boguests, bonelesses, Peg-powlers, pucks, fays, kidnappers, gally-beggars, hudskins, nickers, madcaps, trolls, robinets, friars' lanthorns, silkies, cauld-lads, death-hearses, goblins, hob-headlesses, buggaboes, kows, or cowes, nickies, nacks (necks), waiths, miffies, buckies, gholes, sylphs, guests, swarths, freiths, freits, gy-carlins (Gyre-carling), pigmies, chittifaces, nixies, Jinny-burnt-tails, dudmen, hell-hounds, dopple-gangers, boggleboes, bogies, redmen, portunes, grants, hobbits, hob-goblins, brown-men, cowies, dunnies, wirrikows, alholdes, mannikins, follets, korreds, lubberkins, cluricauns, kobolds, leprechauns, kors, mares, korreds, puckles, korigans, sylvans, succubuses, black-men, shadows, banshees, lianhanshees, clab-bernappers, Gabriel-hounds, mawkins, doubles, corpse lights or candles, scrats, mahounds, trows, gnomes, sprites, fates, fiends, sybils, nick-nevins, whitewomen, fairies, thrummy-caps, cutties, and nisses, and apparitions of every shape, make, form, fashion, kind and description, that there was not a village in England that had not its own peculiar ghost. Nay, every lone tenement, castle, or mansion-house, which could boast of any antiquity had its bogle, its spectre, or its knocker. The churches, churchyards, and cross-roads, were all haunted. Every green lane had its boulder-stone on which an apparition kept watch at night. Every common had its circle of fairies belonging to it. And there was scarcely a shepherd to be met with who had not seen a spirit!

The Departure of the Fairies

From the time of Chaucer onwards, the fairies have been said to have departed or to be in decline, but still they linger. Some 200 years later, Bishop Richard Corbet pursues the same theme:

> Farewell rewards and fairies,
> Good housewives now may say;
> For now foul sluts in dairies
> Do fare as well as they.
>
> And though they sweep their hearths no less
> Than maids were wont to do,
> Yet who of late for cleanliness
> Finds sixpence in her shoe?

A little later Aubrey has a story of a fairy driven away when bells were hung in Inkberrow Church. He was heard lamenting:

> 'Neither sleep, neither lie,
> Inkberrow's ting-tang hangs so high.'

Some two centuries later, Ruth Tongue picked up a similar story in Somerset, to be found in *County Folk-Lore* (vol. VIII, p. 117). It was about the farmer of Knighton Farm on Exmoor, who was on very friendly terms with the pixies. They used to thresh his corn for him and do all manner of odd jobs, until his wife, full of good-will, left suits of clothes for them, and of course, like brownies, they had to leave. But they did not lose their kindly feeling for the farmer, and one day, after the Withypool bells were hung, the pixy father met him.

'Wilt gie us the lend of thy plough and tackle?' he said.

The farmer was cautious – he'd heard how the pixies used horses.

'What vor do 'ee want'n?' he asked.

'I d'want to take my good wife and littlings out of the noise of they ding-dongs.' The farmer trusted the pixies, and they moved, lock, stock and barrel over to Winsford Hill, and when the old pack horses trotted home they looked like beautiful two-year-olds.

Somewhere at the beginning of the nineteenth century, Hugh Miller recorded what was supposed to be the final departure of the fairies from Scotland at Burn of Eathie. It is to be found in *The Old Red Sandstone* as a footnote in Chapter 11.

On a Sabbath morning . . . the inmates of this little hamlet had all gone to church, all except a herd-boy, and a little girl, his sister, who were lounging beside one of the cottages; when, just as the shadow of the garden-dial had fallen on the line of noon, they saw a long cavalcade ascending out of the ravine through the wooded hollow. It winded among the knolls and bushes; and, turning round the northern gable of the cottage beside which the sole spectators of the scene were stationed, began to ascend the eminence toward the south. The horses were shaggy, diminutive things, speckled dun and grey; the riders, stunted, misgrown, ugly creatures, attired in antique jerkins of plaid, long grey cloaks, and little red caps, from under which their wild uncombed locks shot out over their cheeks and foreheads. The boy and his sister stood gazing in utter dismay and astonishment, as rider after rider, each one more uncouth and dwarfish than the one that had preceded it, passed the cottage, and disappeared among the brushwood which at that period covered the hill, until at length the entire rout, except the last rider, who lingered a few yards behind the others, had gone by. 'What are ye, little mannie? and where are ye going?' inquired the boy, his curiosity getting the better of his fears and his prudence. 'Not of the race of Adam,' said the creature, turning for a moment in his saddle: 'the People of Peace shall never more be seen in Scotland.'

Aberdeenshire is in the Northern Lowlands; the Highlanders would not so easily bid the fairies farewell.

Indeed, in all the Celtic parts of Britain living traditions still linger. Even in the Midlands, in Oxfordshire, A. J. Evans, writing about the Rollright Stones in the *Folk-Lore Journal* of 1895, gives the last recorded tradition of the fairies. An old man, Will Hughes, recently dead when Evans wrote, claimed to have seen them dancing round the King Stone. They came out of a hole in the ground near it. Betsy Hughes, his widow, knew the hole: she and her playmates used to put a stone over it, to keep the fairies from coming out when they were playing there.

Yet, however often they may be reported as gone, the fairies still linger. In Ireland the fairy beliefs are still part of the normal texture of life; in the Highlands and Islands the traditions continue. Not only in the Celtic areas, but all over England scattered fairy anecdotes are always turning up. Like the chorus of policemen in *The Pirates of Penzance*, they say, 'We go, we go,' but they don't go.

Fairy Funerals

Alan Cunningham in his *Lives of Eminent British Painters* (pp. 228–9) records that William Blake claimed to have seen a fairy funeral. 'Did you ever see a fairy's funeral, madam?' said Blake to a lady who happened to sit next to him. 'Never, Sir!' said the lady. 'I have,' said Blake, 'but not before last night.' And he went on to tell how, in his garden, he had seen 'a procession of creatures of the size and colour of green and grey grasshoppers, bearing a body laid out on a rose-leaf, which they buried with songs, and then disappeared'.

Most people would deny the possibility of a fairy funeral, believing the fairies to have lives co-terminous with this earthly world, or else that they dwindle and disappear in the course of ages, like the small people of Cornwall. Yet, here and there, people claim, like Blake, to have seen fairy funerals. One of these is preserved in the archives of the School of Scottish Studies among the fairy experiences of Walter Johnstone, one of the travelling people of Perthshire. He found a ruined house near Tom na Toul with a well near it. He was just going to dip his can into the well when he saw a light coming out of the bushes. Two wee men came out, about six inches tall, carrying a coffin between them. They were wearing bowler hats, not the 'lum hats' usually worn at Scottish funerals. Dr T. F. G. Paterson of Armagh Museum collected a similar account from one of the old people:

A man once followed a fairy funeral. He was up late at night an' heard the convoy comin'. He slipped out an' followed them an' they disappeared into Lisletrim Fort (a triple-ringed fort near Cullyhanna). He heard the noise of them walking plain, but he saw none of them.

Kirk in his incomparable work puts a period to fairy lives and also mentions funerals.

There Men travell much abroad, either presaging or aping the dismall and tragicall Actions of some amongst us; and have also many disastorous Doings of their own, as Convocations, Fighting, Gashes, Wounds, and Buriälls, both in the Earth and Air. They live much longer than wee; yet die at last, or at least vanish from that State.

A little later he says: 'They are not subject to sore Sicknesses, but dwindle and decay at a certain Period, all about ane Age.'

Some people are not certain that their funerals are not part of this 'presaging or aping the dismall and tragicall Actions' of men; at least it is so in Bowker's 'Fairy Funeral', in his *Goblin Tales of Lancashire*. Two men were once walking home towards Langton village on a clear moonlight night. One was the old cow-doctor, Adam, and the other was a lively young fellow called Robin. As they came up to the church the first stroke of twelve sounded and they passed it as the chimes pealed out. A moment later they stopped, for the peal of the passing-bell began to ring. They counted the strokes, and after twenty-six they stopped – Robin was twenty-six years old. They wondered who it could be among his companions, but decided that they would know in the morning, and hurried on towards home. But as they reached the drive and lodge of the ancient abbey, the gate swung open and a little dark figure came out with a red cap on his head. He was waving his arms and singing a sweet but mournful dirge, and he was followed by a procession dressed like him which bore in the midst of it a tiny coffin with the lid pushed back so that the face was visible. The two men drew back into the hedge, but as the coffin passed old Adam leant forward, and in the moonlight saw the face of the corpse. 'Robin, mi lad,' he said, 'it's the picter o' thee as they hev i' the coffin!' Robin started forward, and saw that it was indeed the miniature of his own face. The bell still tolled and the funeral cortège passed on towards the church. Robin took it for a death warning and determined to know the appointed time. Adam tried to restrain him, but he hurried after the feeorin, and, touching the leader, he asked, trembling, 'Winnot yo' tell mi heaw lung I've to live?' At once, with a flash of lightning and a spatter of rain, the whole procession vanished, and the two men made their way homeward as best they could through wind and rain.

From that time Robin was a changed man. There was no more riot and merriment for him. His only comfort was to sit with old Adam at night and talk over what they had seen and heard. In a month's time he fell from a stack and was fatally injured.

This is the fullest account of a warning funeral, but there are reports of them in Galloway and Wales. The Welsh corpse-candles are among the will o' the wisp phenomena discussed by Aubrey and Sikes, but these are ascribed to the spirits of the dead rather than to the fairies.

The funeral of a genuine fairy, indeed the Fairy Queen, is described by Hunt in *Popular Romances of the West of England* (p. 102). This is a shortened version of his tale.

One night an old man called Richard was returning home late with a load of fish from St Ives when he heard the bell of Lelant Church tolling out, with a heavy, muffled sound, and saw a light from the windows. He drew near and peered in. The church was brightly lighted, and a crowd of little people were moving along the central aisle, with a bier carried between six of them. The body was uncovered; it was as small as the tiniest doll, and of waxen beauty. The mourners were carrying flowering myrtle in their hands, and wearing wreaths of small roses. A little grave had been dug near the altar. The body was lowered into it, and the fairies threw their flowers after, crying aloud: 'Our queen is dead!' When one of the little grave-diggers threw in a shovelful of earth so dismal a cry arose that Richard echoed it. At once the lights went out, and the fairies rushed past him like a swarm of bees, piercing him with sharp points. Richard fled in terror, and thought himself lucky to have escaped with his life.

It is notable that these fairies, though they showed the normal dislike of prying intruders, and hence of an infringement of fairy privacy, were undeterred by crucifix or consecration.

Poems, Tales and Reports

The Faiery Dance

In the year 1633–4, soone after I had entered into my grammar at the Latin Schoole at Yatton Keynel, (near Chippenham, Wilts.), our curate Mr Hart, was annoy'd one night by these elves or fayries. Comming over the downes, it being neere darke, and approaching one of the faiery dances, as the common people call them in these parts, viz. the greene circles made by those sprites on the grasse, he all at once sawe an innumerable quantitie of pigmies or very small people, dancing rounde and rounde, and singing, and making all maner of small odd noyses. He, being very greatly amaz'd, and yet not being able, as he sayes, to run away from them, being, as he supposes, kept there in a kind of enchantment, they no sooner perceave him but they surround him on all sides, and what betwixt feare and amazement, he fell down scarcely knowing what he did; and thereupon these little creatures pinch'd him all over, and made a sorte of quick humming noyse all the time; but at length they left him, and when the sun rose, he found himself exactly in the midst of one of these faiery dances. This relation I had from him myselfe, a few days after he was so tormented; but when I and my bedfellow Stump wente soon afterwards, at night time to the dances on the downes, we saw none of the elves or faieries. But indeede it is saide they seldom appeare to any persons who go to seeke for them.

John Aubrey, (1626–97)

The Boggart

There was once a Yorkshire farmer called George Gilbertson whose house was much tormented by a boggart. He played his tricks on everyone about the house, and especially on the children. He would snatch away their bread and butter and upset their porringers and shove them into corners and cupboards; and yet not a glimpse of him was ever seen. There was an elf-bore in one of the cupboards, a hole where a knot of wood had been, and one day the youngest boy stuck an old shoehorn into it. It was pushed back so hard that it popped out of the hole and hit him on the forehead. After this the children loved to play with the boggart by thrusting sticks into the hole and seeing them shot back. But the boggart's tricks got worse and worse, and poor Mrs Gilbertson became so anxious for the children that at last they decided to move. So on the day of the flitting their nearest neighbour, John Marshall, saw them following their last creaking carts out of the empty yard.

'And so you're flitting at last, Georgie?' he said.

'Aye, Johnny lad, I'm forced tull it; for that domned boggart torments us soa we can neaither rest neet nor day for't. It seems to have sech a malice against t' poor bairns that it omost kills my poor dame at thowt on't. And soa ye see we're forced to flit like.'

A sudden unexpected echo to his words came in a deep voice out of the old upright churn in the last cart.

'Aye, Johnny lad, we're flitting, ye see.'

'It's the domned boggart!' said George. 'If I'd a knowed thou'd been there I hadn't a stirred a leg. Turn back, Mally,' he said to his wife. 'We mun as well be tormented in t'owd house as in another that's not to our liking.'

So back they went; and the boggart played about their farm till he was tired of the sport.

Yorkshire

The Bogie's Field

Once there was a bogie that laid claim to a farmer's field. The farmer did not think it fair; but after a long argument they decided that, though the farmer should do the work, they should divide the produce between them. So the first year in spring the farmer said: 'Which will you have, tops or bottoms?'

'Bottoms,' said the bogie.

So the farmer planted wheat; all the bogie got was stubble and roots. Next year he said he would have tops, and the farmer planted turnips; so he was no better off than before. He began to think he was getting the worst of it; so the next year he said: 'You'll plant wheat, and we'll have a mowing match, and him who wins shall have it for keeps.' 'Agreed,' said the farmer, and they divided the field up into two equal halves. A little before the corn ripened, however, the farmer went to the smith and ordered some hundreds of thin iron rods, which he stuck all over the bogie's half of the field. The farmer got on like a house on fire, but the poor bogie kept muttering to himself, 'Darnation hard docks, 'nation hard docks!' and his scythe grew so blunt that it would hardly cut butter. After about an hour he called to the farmer, 'When do we wiffle-waffle, mate?' for in a match all the reapers whet their scythes together.

'Waffle?' said the farmer. 'Oh, about noon, maybe.'

'Noon!' said the bogie. 'Then I've lost,' and off he went, and troubled the farmer no more.

Northamptonshire

Ethna the Bride

Finvarra, or Fin Bheara, the Irish fairy king who was also king of the dead, though he had a beautiful queen of his own, was amorous of mortal women, and any woman who was renowned for her beauty stood in special danger from him. Lady Wilde in her *Ancient Legends of Ireland* tells of one Ethna the Bride who was said to be the most beautiful woman then in Ireland and who was stolen by Finvarra. Ethna was newly married, and the young lord her husband was so proud of her beauty that he held festivities day after day. His castle was near the fairy hill which covered Finvarra's palace, but they had been long friends, and from time to time he set out offerings of wine to the fairy king, so he had no fear of him. Nevertheless one evening, as Ethna was floating through the dance, shining like moonlight in her silver dress, her hand slipped from her partner's and she fell to the ground in a swoon. Nothing would revive her, and they carried her to bed where she lay motionless. In the morning she seemed to revive, but would speak of nothing but a beautiful country which she had visited, and to which she longed to return. At night she sank deep again into sleep. Her old nurse was set to guard her, but in the silence of the night she too fell asleep, and when she woke at sunrise Ethna had gone. The whole castle was roused, and they searched high and low, but no sight, sound nor trace of her was to be found. It was clear that the fairies had some part in her disappearance, and the young lord rode off at top speed to Knock-Ma under which his friend Finvarra lived, to seek his counsel as to how to find her. When he reached the Rath he dismounted, and had begun to climb its slope when he heard voices above him in the air. 'Finvarra is happy now,' said one, 'when he has carried Ethna the Bride into his palace. Her husband will never see her again.' 'Yet he could win her back,' said another, 'if he could dig a deep hole down into the heart of the Rath and let the light of day into it; but he will never win his way down, for Finvarra is more powerful than any mortal man.' 'Yet I will conquer him,' thought the young lord; and he sent for workmen far and wide and they dug down into the hill, a deep, wide trench, so that when darkness fell they thought that their task was more than half done, and that they would reach Finvarra's palace by the next day. So they went to rest in high hopes. But next morning the trench was gone, and the grass grew over the hill as if it had never been disturbed. Then most men despaired, but the young lord had a brave heart, and he added more diggers to the many who were working, and that day they got even deeper than the day before, but the next morning all trace of their labour had disappeared. And the third morning it was the same again. Then the young lord was ready to die for grief, when he heard a voice in the air above him saying 'Sprinkle the earth with salt and your work will be safe.' Hope sprang up again in his heart, and he sent round and gathered salt from all his people, and that night they covered all the piles of earth with salt before they left them. Next morning their work had been untouched, and they set to work with a good heart, and before the day was over they were so near to Fairyland that when they put their ears to the clay they could hear fairy music, and voices speaking. And one voice said: 'Finvarra is sad now, for he knows that if one human spade cuts into his palace wall it will crumble into dust.' Another answered: 'But if the king sends Ethna back to her lord, we shall all be saved.' Then the voice of Finvarra rang out: 'Lay down your spades, men of earth, and at sunset Ethna shall return to her lord.' At that the lord told his men to stop digging, and at sunset he rode up to the mouth of the Glen, and Ethna came walking up the deep cleft, shining like silver, and he snatched her up to his horse's back and rode with her to his castle; but Finvarra had played him false, for when he carried her in she lay in his arms without speech or movement, and when they laid her on the bed she lay there like a waxen image and nothing would rouse her, so that they began to fear that she had eaten fairy food and that her soul had remained in Fairyland. One night as the lord was riding sadly home he heard the friendly voices in the air. And one said: 'It is a year and a day since Ethna came home to her lord, and still she lies motionless, for Finvarra has her soul with him still in his palace under Knock-Ma.' And the other answered: 'Yet her husband could win her back to mortal life if he undid the girdle round her waist and took out the fairy pin with which it is fastened. If he burned the girdle and sprinkled the ashes outside her door, and buried the pin in the earth, then her human soul would come back to her.' The young lord turned his horse, and rode back like lightning. With great difficulty he untangled the girdle and disengaged the fairy pin. He burnt the girdle and scattered the ashes outside the door. Still she never moved. Then he took the pin and buried it under a fairy thorn where no one would disturb it. When he came back, Ethna sat up in bed and stretched out her arms to him. She knew and remembered everything, except that the year she had spent in Fairyland was like the dream of a single night. Finvarra never troubled them again, and they lived out their mortal lives in great happiness. They have long gone, but the deep cleft is still left in Knock-Ma, and is still called the Fairy Glen.

Ireland

The Demon Dancers

Four young men were on a hunting trip and spent the night in an empty shieling, a hut built to give shelter for the sheep in the grazing season. They began to dance, one supplying mouth-music. One of the dancers wished that they had partners. Almost at once four women came in. Three danced, the fourth stood by the music-maker. But as he hummed he saw drops of blood falling from the dancers and he fled out of the shieling, pursued by his demon partner. He took refuge among the horses and she could not get to him, probably because of the iron with which they were shod. But she circled round him all night, and only disappeared when the sun rose. He went back into the shieling and found the bloodless bodies of the dancers lying there. Their partners had sucked them dry.

Ross-shire

St Collen and the Fairy King

St Collen, after three years at Glastonbury, had been elected abbot, but he soon renounced his abbacy for the heavier and harder life of a hermit, and found a cell at the foot of Glastonbury Tor. As he was meditating in it one day he heard two men saying that Gwyn ap Nudd, king of Annwn, had his castle on the top of the Tor. St Collen stuck his head out of the window and rebuked them for talking in such good terms of devils from Hell. The men warned him not to talk in that way of Gwyn ap Nudd, or it would be the worse for him. But Collen persisted. A few days later a messenger came to the cell inviting Collen to visit the fairy king. Collen refused, but day after day the invitation was repeated, and at last the messenger lost patience and said that it would be the worse for him if he did not come. Collen went with him, but he picked up a stoup of holy water and hid it under his cassock.

At the top of the Tor he found the most beautiful castle that the mind of man could conceive, troops of bodyguards and a number of musicians with all kinds of instruments, bevies of maidens, and gallant young men riding around on beautiful horses. He was conducted into the banqueting hall where the king pressed him courteously to sit down and eat. A great banquet was carried in by fair pages in uniforms of scarlet and blue. 'Eat and drink,' said the king, 'and if this does not please you, there is plenty more of all sorts.' But Collen, whose eyes were not blinded by glamour, replied, 'I do not eat the leaves of a tree.' A shudder ran through the shining assembly, but the king still spoke courteously: 'Tell me, have you ever seen attendants better dressed than my pages in their fair liveries of scarlet and blue?' 'They are suitably dressed,' said Collen, 'for what they are.' 'And what is that?' said the king. 'Scarlet is for the ever-living flames,' Collen replied, 'and blue for the eternal ice of Hell.' With that he dashed the holy water over them all. The gorgeous show vanished in a minute, and Collen found himself standing in the pale light of dawn among the grassy tumps at the summit of the Tor.

Welsh origin

The Fairy Bathers of Ilkley Wells

William Butterfield . . . always opened the door the first thing in the morning, and he did this without ever noticing anything out of the common until one beautiful quiet mid-summer morning. As he ascended the brow of the hill he noticed rather particularly how the birds sang so sweetly, and cheerily, and vociferously, making the valley echo with the music of their voices. And in thinking it over afterwards he remembered noticing them, and considered this sign attributable to the after-incident. As he drew near the Wells he took out of his pocket the massive iron key, and placed it in the lock; but there was something 'canny' about it, and instead of the key lifting the lever it only turned round and round in the lock. He drew the key back to see that it was all right, and declared 'it was the same that he had on the previous night hung up behind his own door down at home'. Then he endeavoured to push the door open, and no sooner did he push it slightly ajar than it was as quickly pushed back again. At last, with one supreme effort, he forced it perfectly open, and back it flew with a great bang! Then whirr, whirr, whirr, such a noise and sight! all over the water and dipping into it was a lot of little creatures, all dressed in green from head to foot, none of them more than eighteen inches high, and making a chatter and jabber thoroughly unintelligible. They seemed to be taking a bath, only they bathed with all their clothes on. Soon, however, one or two of them began to make off, bounding over the walls like squirrels. Finding they were all making ready for decamping, and wanting to have a word with them, he shouted at the top of his voice – indeed, he declared afterwards he couldn't find anything else to say or do – 'Hallo there!' Then away the whole tribe went, helter skelter, toppling and tumbling, heads over heels, heels over heads, and all the while making a noise not unlike a disturbed nest of young partridges. The sight was so unusual that he declared he either couldn't or daren't attempt to rush after them. He stood as still and confounded, he said, as old Jeremiah Lister down there at Wheatley did, half a century previous, when a witch from Ilkley put an ash riddle upon the side of the river Wharfe, and sailed across in it to where he was standing. When the well had got quite clear of these strange beings he ran to the door and looked to see where they had fled, but nothing was to be seen. He ran back into the bath to see if they had left anything behind; but there was nothing; the water lay still and clear as he had left it on the previous night. He thought they might perhaps have left some of their clothing behind in their haste, but he could find none, and so he gave up looking, and commenced his usual routine of preparing the baths; not, however, without trotting to the door once or twice to see if they might be coming back; but he saw them no more.

Yorkshire

The Broken Ped

A farm labourer whose way took him across Wick Moor heard the sound of someone crying. It was someone small, and within a few steps he came across a child's ped (spade or shovel) broken in half. Being a kindly father himself, he stopped and took a few moments to mend it neatly and strongly, never noticing that he was standing close to the barrow called 'Pixy Mound'.

Putting down the mended ped, he called out, 'There 'tis then – never cry no more,' and went on his way.

On his return from work the ped was gone, and a fine new-baked cake lay in its place.

Despite the warnings of his comrade, the man ate it and found it 'proper good'. Saying so loudly, he called out, 'Good night to 'ee,' and prospered ever after.

Somerset

From *The Wife of Bath's Tale*

In th'olde dayes of the King Arthour,
Of which that Britons speken greet honour,
Al was this land fulfild of faierie.
The elf-queene, with hir joly compaignie,
Daunced ful ofte in many a grene mede.
This was the olde opinion, as I rede;
I speke of manie hundred yeres ago.
But now kan no man se none elves mo,
For now the grete charitee and prayeres
Of limitours and othere hooly freres,
That serchen every lond and every streem,
As thikke as motes in the sonne-beem,
Blessinge halles, chambres, kichenes, boures,
Citees, burghes, castels, hye toures,
Thropes, bernes, shipnes, daieries –
This maketh that ther ben no faieries.
For ther as wont to walken was an elf,
Ther walketh now the limitour himself,

In undermeles and in morweninges,
And seyth his matins and his hooly thinges
As he gooth in his limitacioun.
Wommen may go now saufly up and doun.
In every bussh or under every tree
Ther is noon oother incubus but he,
And he ne wol doon hem but dishonour.

Geoffrey Chaucer (c.1340–1400)

The Lothian Farmer's Wife

The wife of a farmer in Lothian had been carried off by the fairies, and, during the year of probation, repeatedly appeared on Sunday, in the midst of her children, combing their hair. On one of these occasions she was accosted by her husband; when she related to him the unfortunate event which had separated them, instructed him by what means he might *win* her, and exhorted him to exert all his courage, since her temporal and eternal happiness depended on the success of his attempt. The farmer, who ardently loved his wife, set out on Hallowe'en, and, in the midst of a plot of furze, waited impatiently for the procession of the fairies. At the ringing of the fairy bridles, and the wild, unearthly sound which accompanied the cavalcade, his heart failed him, and he suffered the ghostly train to pass by without interruption. When the last had rode past, the whole troop vanished, with loud shouts of laughter and exultation; among which he plainly discovered the voice of his wife, lamenting that he had lost her for ever.

Lothian

The Red-Haired Man

In the Irish tales there are many examples of a 'red-haired man' who intervenes to rescue people enticed into Fairyland, and who is supposed to be a mortal captive there. One example is perhaps enough, drawn from Lady Wilde's *Ancient Legends of Ireland* (vol. 1, pp. 54–6). It is about a girl who was enticed into a fairy dance, and, after dancing with the prince, she was led down to a gorgeous banquet:

She took the golden cup the prince handed to her, and raised it to her lips to drink. Just then a man passed close to her, and whispered –

'Eat no food, and drink no wine, or you will never reach your home again.'

So she laid down the cup, and refused to drink. On this they were angry, and a great noise arose, and a fierce, dark man stood up, and said –

'Whoever comes to us must drink with us.'

And he seized her arm, and held the wine to her lips, so that she almost died of fright. But at that moment a red-haired man came up, and he took her by the hand and led her out.

'You are safe for this time,' he said. 'Take this herb, and hold it in your hand till you reach home, and no one can harm you.'

And he gave her a branch of the plant called *Athair-Luss* (the ground ivy).

This she took, and fled away along the sward in the dark night: but all the time she heard footsteps behind her in pursuit. At last she reached home and barred the door, and went to bed, when a great clamour arose outside, and voices were heard crying to her –

'The power we have over you is gone through the magic of the herb; but wait – when you dance again to the music on the hill, you will stay with us for evermore, and none shall hinder.'

However, she kept the magic branch safely, and the fairies never troubled her more; but it was long and long before the sound of the fairy music left her ears which she had danced to that November night on the hillside with her fairy lover.

Ireland

Cherry of Zennor

Cherry was one of a large family living in Zennor, a small village in Cornwall, and when she got to the age of fourteen it was time for her to go out into the world. She set out to be hired at the local fair, but her courage failed her, and on the Lady Downs she sat down and cried. Whilst she was still weeping a handsome, well-dressed gentleman stood beside her, and asked what was troubling her. After some conversation he said that he was going out to hire a neat, tidy girl to look after his little son, because he had recently been left a widower. He praised Cherry's neatly-mended clothes and tidy looks, and hired her to go along with him. They went an immense way, down and down twisting lanes with high hedges closing above them. The gentleman lifted Cherry over several streams and at length they came to a gate into a garden where flowers of all seasons grew and flowered together. Birds were singing all round them, and Cherry thought she had never seen so lovely a place. A little sharp-eyed boy ran out to greet them, followed by an old, cross-looking woman. 'That's my wife's mother,' said the gentleman, 'but she will only stay a few days to put you in the ways of the place, and then she shall go.' The old woman looked crossly at Cherry and took her in, muttering that she knew Robin would choose a fool. It was a strange place, with long passages and a big room locked up, into which the old woman led Cherry. It was full of what Cherry thought of as dead people – presumably statues – and there was a coffin-like box in the middle of the room which Cherry was set to polish. When she rubbed it hard it made a strange, groaning sound, and Cherry fell down in a faint. Her master ran in, picked her up and took her out, kissed and comforted her, and sent the old woman away.

Cherry's duties were very light and pleasant; she had to play with the little boy, milk a cow who appeared mysteriously when she was called, and anoint the little boy's eyes every morning with green ointment. The pleasantest of her duties was to help her master work in the garden. At the end of every row he gave Cherry a kiss, and she would have been very happy there if it had not been that her master disappeared for many hours together, and when he came back went into the locked room from which strange sounds proceeded. Her little charge would answer none of her questions, but only said 'I'll tell

Grannie', if she asked him anything; but she fancied that he saw much more than she did, and his eyes were very bright; so one morning she sent him off to pick some flowers and slyly put a crumb of the ointment in her own eye. This produced a transformation: the garden was swarming with little creatures. Her eyes smarted and she ran to the well to wash out the ointment. At the bottom of the well she saw numbers of tiny people dancing, and to her fury she saw her master among them, as tiny as they were, and on very familiar terms with the little fairy ladies. Soon she saw her master coming back as his normal size. He went up to the locked room and went inside. Cherry followed him and peeped through the keyhole. He lifted the lid of the coffin and a lady came out, sat down, and began to play upon the coffin, and all the statues began to dance. Cherry ran away weeping, and when her master called her to weed the garden with him, she was very sulky. At the end of the first row he tried to kiss her, but she pushed him away saying: 'Go and kiss your little midgets at the bottom of the well.' Her master looked very sad. 'Cherry, you have been using the ointment that you were told not to use. I am sorry, but you must go home, and old Grace must come back again.' Cherry cried and besought, but he made her pack her clothes, and led her back by the long uphill way on to the Lady Downs. She never saw him again, and like many people who have visited Fairyland, she did no good in the mortal world, but hung about the Lady Downs hoping Robin her master would come back and see her.

Cornwall

True Thomas

True Thomas lay oer yond grassy bank,
   And he beheld a ladie gay,
A ladie that was brisk and bold,
   Come riding oer the fernie brae.

Her skirt was of the grass-green silk,
   Her mantel of the velvet fine,
At ilka tett of her horse's mane
   Hung fifty silver bells and nine.

True Thomas he took off his hat,
   And bowed him low down till his knee:
'All hail, thou mighty Queen of Heaven!
   For your peer on earth I never did see.'

'O no, O no, True Thomas,' she says,
   'That name does not belong to me;
I am but the queen of fair Elfland,
   And I'm come here for to visit thee.

'But ye maun go wi me now, Thomas,
    True Thomas, ye maun go wi me,
For ye maun serve me seven years,
    Thro weel or wae as may chance to be.'

She turned about her milk-white steed,
    And took True Thomas up behind,
And aye wheneer her bridle rang,
    The steed flew swifter than the wind.

For forty days and forty nights
    He wade thro red blude to the knee,
And he saw neither sun nor moon,
    But heard the roaring of the sea.

O they rade on, and further on,
    Until they came to a garden green:
'Light down, light down, ye ladie free,
    Some of that fruit let me pull to thee.'

'O no, O no, True Thomas,' she says,
    'That fruit maun not be touched by thee,
For a' the plagues that are in hell
    Light on the fruit of this countrie.

'But I have a loaf here in my lap,
    Likewise a bottle of claret wine,
And now ere we go farther on,
    We'll rest a while, and ye may dine.'

When he had eaten and drunk his fill,
    'Lay down your head upon my knee,'
The lady sayd, 'ere we climb yon hill,
    And I will show you fairlies three.

'O see not ye yon narrow road,
    So thick beset wi thorns and briers?
That is the path of righteousness,
    Tho after it but few enquires.

'And see not ye that braid braid road,
    That lies across yon lillie leven?
That is the path of wickedness,
    Tho some call it the road to heaven.

'And see not ye that bonny road,
    Which winds about the fernie brae?
That is the road to fair Elfland,
    Where you and I this night maun gae.

'But Thomas, ye maun hold your tongue,
   Whatever you may hear or see,
For gin ae word you should chance to
      speak,
   You will neer get back to your ain
   countrie.'

He has gotten a coat of the even cloth,
   And a pair of shoes of velvet green,
And till seven years were past and gone
   True Thomas on earth was never seen.

Ballad (collected in the Nineteenth Century)

The Chessmen of Lewis

In 1831 a high tide on the coast near Uig in the Isle of Lewis washed away a sand-bank and exposed a cave in which there was a small beehive-shaped building rather like the little domestic grinding querns to be found in the Highlands. A labourer working near found it, and, thinking it might contain some treasure, broke into it. He found a cache of eighty-four carved chessmen ranged together. They had an uncanny look, and he flung down his spade and ran, convinced that he had come on a sleeping company of fairies. His wife was of sterner stuff and made him go back and fetch them. The greater part of them are now in the British Museum. Replicas have been made of them, but the originals, all mustered together, are much more impressive. A tradition has arisen about them. It is said that the guards who take the guard-dogs round at night cannot get them to pass the Celtic chessmen. They bristle and drag back on their haunches. So perhaps the Highlander's superstition can be excused.

The Fairy Cup

In the province of the Deiri (Yorkshire), not far from my birth-place, a wonderful thing occurred, which I have known from my boyhood. There is a town a few miles distant from the Eastern Sea, near which are those celebrated waters commonly called Gipse ... A peasant of this town went once to see a friend who lived in the next town, and it was late at night when he was coming back, not very sober; when lo! from the adjoining barrow, which I have often seen, and which is not much over a quarter of a mile from the town, he heard the voices of people singing, and, as it were, joyfully feasting. He wondered who they could be that were breaking in that place, by their merriment, the silence of the dead night, and he wished to examine into the matter more closely. Seeing a door open in the side of the barrow, he went up to it, and looked in; and there he beheld a large and luminous house, full of people, women as well as men, who were reclining as at a solemn banquet. One of the attendants, seeing him standing at the door, offered him a cup. He took it, but would not drink; and pouring out the contents, kept the vessel. A great tumult arose at the banquet on account of his taking away the cup, and all the guests pursued him; but he escaped by the fleetness of the beast he rode, and got into the town with his booty. Finally, this vessel of unknown material, of unusual colour, and of extraordinary form, was presented to Henry the Elder, king of the English, as a valuable gift, and was then given to the queen's brother David, king of the Scots, and was kept for several years in the treasury of Scotland; and a few years ago (as I have heard from good authority), it was given by William, king of the Scots, to Henry the Second, who wished to see it.

William of Newbridge (Twelfth Century)

The Fairy Dwelling on Selena Moor

The tale is about a Mr Noy, a well-liked farmer, who
lived near Selena Moor and who went out to the neighbouring inn one night to order drink for the Harvest
Home next day. He left the inn, but never arrived home.
They searched for him for three days, and at last, passing
within half a mile of his home, they heard dogs howling,
and a horse neighing. They went over the treacherous
bogland of the moor, and found a great thicket, where
Mr Noy's horse was tethered, with the dogs beside it. The
horse had fed well on the rich grass, but the dogs were
very thin. The horse led them to a ruined bowjey (or barn)
and there they found Mr Noy fast asleep. He was surprised
to see that it was morning already, and was very dazed
and bewildered, but at last they got his story from him.
He had made a short-cut through the moor, but had lost
his way and had wandered, he thought, many miles over
country unknown to him, until he saw lights in the distance
and heard music. He hurried towards it, thinking that he
had come at last to a farmhouse, where they were perhaps

holding a Harvest Home supper. His horse and dogs shrank back and would not come with him, so he tied his horse to a thorn, and went on through a most beautiful orchard towards a house, outside which he saw hundreds of people either dancing or sitting drinking at tables. They were all richly dressed, but they looked to him very small, and their benches and tables and cups were small too. Quite close to him stood a girl in white, taller than the rest, and playing a kind of tambourine. The tunes were lively, and the dancers were the nimblest he had ever seen. Soon the girl gave the tambourine to an old fellow near, and went into the house to fetch out a black-jack of ale for the company. Mr Noy, who loved dancing and would have been glad of a drink, drew near to the corner of the house, but the girl met his eyes, and signed to him to keep back. She spoke a few words to the old fellow with the tambourine, and then came towards him.

'Follow me into the orchard,' she said.

She went before him to a sheltered place, and there in the quiet starlight, away from the dazzle of the candles, he recognized her as Grace Hutchens, who had been his sweetheart for a long time, but had died, or was thought to have died, three or four years before.

'Thank the stars, dear William,' she said, 'that I was

on the look-out to stop ye, or ye would this minute be changed into the small people's state, like I am, woe is me!'

He would have kissed her, but she warned him anxiously against touching her, and against eating a fruit or plucking a flower if he wished ever to reach his home again.

'For eating a tempting plum in this enchanted orchard was my undoing,' she said. 'You may think it strange, but it was all through my love for you that I am come to this. People believed, and so it seemed, that I was found on the moor dead; what was buried for me, however, was only a changeling or a sham body, never mine, I should think, for it seems to me that I feel much the same still as when I lived to be your sweetheart.'

As she said this several little voices squeaked, 'Grace, Grace, bring us more beer and cider, be quick, be quick!'

'Follow me into the garden, and remain there behind the house; be sure you keep out of sight, and don't for your life touch fruit or flower.'

Mr Noy begged her to bring him a drink of cider too, but she said she would not on his life; and she soon returned, and led him into a bowery walk, where all kinds of flowers were blooming, and told him how she came there. One evening about dusk she was out on Selena Moor looking for a stray sheep, when she heard Mr Noy hallooing to his dogs, so she took a short-cut towards him, and got lost in a place where the ferns were above her head, and so wandered on for hours until she came to an orchard where music was sounding, but though the music was sometimes quite near she could not get out of the orchard, but wandered round as if she was pixy-led. At length, worn out with hunger and thirst, she plucked a beautiful golden plum from one of the trees, and began to eat it. It dissolved into bitter water in her mouth, and she fell to the ground in a faint. When she revived she found herself surrounded by a crowd of little people, who laughed and rejoiced at getting a neat girl to bake and brew for them and to look after their mortal babies, who were not so strong, they said, as they used to be in the old days.

She said their lives seemed unnatural and a sham. 'They have little sense or feeling; what serves them in a way as such, is merely the remembrance of whatever pleased them when they lived as mortals – maybe thousands of years ago. What appear like ruddy apples and other delicious fruit are only sloes, hoggins (haws) and blackberries.'

Mr Noy asked her if any fairy babies were born, and

she answered that just occasionally a fairy child was born, and then there was great rejoicing – every little fairy man, however old and wizened, was proud to be thought its father. 'For you must remember that they are not of our religion,' she said in answer to his surprised look, 'but star-worshippers. They don't always live together like Christians and turtle-doves; considering their long existence, such constancy would be tiresome for them; anyhow, the small tribe seem to think so.'

She told him also that she was now more content with her condition, since she was able to take the form of a small bird and fly about near him.

When she was called away again Mr Noy thought he might find a way to rescue them both; so he took his hedging gloves out of his pocket, turned them inside out and threw them among the fairies. Immediately all vanished, Grace and all, and he found himself standing alone in the ruined bowjey.

Cornwall

Fairies on the Eastern Green

During the evening, after much coaxing, our host told the story which his wife had spoken of as a true one; telling how a company of smugglers, of his acquaintance, had been driven away from Market-jew Green by small-folks (fairies).

There is some hope that all the fairy-folk have not yet entirely forsaken this neighbourhood, as there are persons now living who have seen them dancing and holding their revels on the Eastern Green within the last fifty years. At that time, however, there were many acres of grass-grown sandy banks there; and a broad belt of soft greensward, which skirted the carriage road, afforded a pleasant walk from Chyannour to Market-jew bridge. Great part of this green has now been swept away by the waves, and much of what the sea spared has been enclosed by the grasping owners of adjacent land, though their right to this ancient common is very questionable.

The following fairy adventure was told to me a short

time since by a grave elderly man who heard it related by the principal person concerned in it.

Tom Warren of Paul, was noted as one of the boldest smugglers round. On a summer's night, about forty years ago, he and five other men landed a boat-load of smuggled goods at a short distance from Long Rock. The brandy, salt, etc., having been taken above high-water mark, two of the men departed for Market-jew, where their best customers lived, and one went over to Newtown to procure horses that the goods might be secured before daybreak.

Tom and the other two, being very tired, lay down by a heap of goods, hoping to get a doze while their comrades were away. They were soon disturbed, however, by the shrill 'tweeting' of 'feapers' (slit quills or reeds, which give a shrill note when blown in). Besides there was a constant tinkling, just like old women make by rattling pewter plates or brass pans to frighten their swarming bees home, or to make them settle.

The men thought this noise might be from a company of young folks keeping up a dance on the Green till a very late hour. Tom went to see who they were and to send them home, for it wasn't desirable for everybody to pry into the fair traders' business. Having passed the beach, he mounted a high sand-bank to have a look round, as the music seemed very near.

At a little distance, in hollows, between sand-banks, he saw glimmering lights, and persons like gaily dressed dolls skipping about and whirling round. Going nearer, he beheld, perched on a pretty high bank in their midst, a score or so of little, old-looking chaps; many of them blew mouth-organs (Pan's pipes); some beat cymbals or tambourines; whilst others played on jew's-harps, or tweeted on May whistles and feapers.

Tom noticed that the little men were rigged all in green, except for their scarlet caps (small people are so fond of that coloured head-gear that they used to be nicknamed 'red-caps'). But what struck him and tickled his fancy most was to see the little, old, grave-looking pipers with their long beards wagging.

In moving their mouths over the reeds, stuck in their breasts, they looked more like buck-goats than anything human, so Tom said; and that for the life of him he couldn't forbear shouting – 'Will e be shaved – will e be shaved old red-caps?' He hailed them twice, and was about to do so again when all the dancers, with scores and hundreds more than he noticed at first sprang up, ranged themselves in rank and file; armed themselves in an instant with bows and arrows, spears and slings; then faced about, looking like vengeance. The band being disposed alongside, played a quick march, and the troops of 'spriggans' stamped on towards Tom, who saw them getting taller as they approached him. Their threatening looks were so frightful that he turned tail and ran down to his comrades, roused them, saying, 'Put to sea for your lives. There's thousands of small people and bucca-boos 'most on our backs! They'll soon surround us!' Tom made off to the boat, and his comrades followed close at his heels; but on the way a shower of pebbles fell on them, and 'burned like coals o' fire wherever they hit them'.

The men pulled many fathoms from shore before they ventured to look up, though they knew themselves safe when on the sea, because none of the fairy tribe dare touch salt water.

At length, casting a glance landward, they saw, ranged along the shore, a company of as ugly-looking creatures as they ever beheld, making threatening gestures and vain endeavours to sling stones at them.

When a furlong or so from land, the men rested on their oars, and kept watching their assailants till near daybreak: then horses being heard galloping along the road from Market-jew, the small people retreated to the sand-banks and the smugglers rowed to land.

Cornwall

The Fairy Banquet

A little mushroome table spred,
After short prayers, they set on bread;
A Moon-parcht grain of purest wheat,
With some small glit'ring gritt, to eate
His choyce bitts with; then in a trice
They make a feast lesse great then nice.

And now, we must imagine first,
The Elves present to quench his thirst
A pure seed-Pearle of Infant dew,
Brought and besweetned in a blew
And pregnant violet; which done,
His kitling eyes begin to runne
Quite through the table, where he spies
The hornes of paperie Butterflies,
Of which he eates, and tastes a little
Of that we call the Cuckoes spittle.
A little Fuz-ball-pudding stands
By, yet not blessed by his hands,
That was too coorse; but then forthwith

He ventures boldly on the pith
Of sugred Rush, and eates the sagge
And well bestrutted Bees sweet bagge:
Gladding his pallat with some store
Of Emits eggs; what wo'd he more?
But Beards of Mice, a Newt's stew'd thigh,
A bloated Earewig, and a Flie;
With the Red-capt worme, that's shut
Within the concave of a Nut,
Browne as his Tooth. A little Moth,
Late fatned in a piece of cloth:
With withered cherries; Mandrakes eares;
Moles eyes; to these, the slain-Stags teares:
The unctuous dewlaps of a Snaile;
The broke-heart of a Nightingale
Ore-come in musicke; with a wine,
Ne're ravisht from the flattering Vine,
But gently prest from the soft side
Of the most sweet and dainty Bride,
Brought in a dainty daizie, which
He fully quaffs up to bewitch
His blood to height; this done, commended
Grace by his Priest; *The feast is ended*.

Robert Herrick, (1591–1674)

The Fairy Spinners

I'm not much of a believer in most of the stories some ones is telling, but after all a body can't help believing a thing they happen to see for themselves.

I remember one winter's night – we were living in a house at the time that was pulled down for the building of the Big Wheel. It was a thatched house with two rooms, and a wall about six foot high dividing them, and from that it was open to the scrabs, or turfs, that were laid across the rafters. My Mother was sitting at the fire busy spinning, and my Father was sitting in the big chair at the end of the table taking a chapter for us out of the Manx Bible. My brother was busy winding a spool and I was working with a bunch of ling, trying to make two or three pegs.

'There's a terrible glisther on to-night,' my Mother said, looking at the fire. 'An' the rain comin' peltin' down the chimley.'

'Yes,' said my Father, shutting the Bible; 'an' we better

get to bed middlin' soon and let the Lil' Ones in to a bit of shelter.'

So we all got ready and went to bed.

Some time in the night my brother wakened me with a: 'Shish! Listen boy, and look at the big light tha's in the kitchen!' Then he rubbed his eyes a bit and whispered: 'What's Mother doin' now at all?'

'Listen!' I said, 'An' you'll hear Mother in bed; it's not her at all; it must be the Little Ones that's agate of the wheel!'

And both of us got frightened, and down with our heads under the clothes and fell asleep. In the morning when we got up we told them what we had seen, first thing.

'Aw, like enough, like enough,' my Father said, looking at the wheel. 'It seems your mother forgot to take the band off last night, a thing people should be careful about, for it's givin' Themselves power over the wheel, an' though their meanin's well enough, the spinnin' they're doin' is nothin' to brag about. The weaver is always shoutin' about their work, an' the bad joinin' they're makin' in the rolls.'

I remember it as well as yesterday – the big light that was at them, and the whirring that was going on. And let anybody say what they like, that's a thing I've seen and heard for myself.

Isle of Man

Yallery Brown

One night a young man called Tom Tiver, as he was going home from work, heard a most distressful crying, like an abandoned child, and made out at last that it came from under a great flat stone, half-buried in the grass, called 'The Strangers' Stone'. He managed to lift it up, and he saw underneath a little thing, the size of a year-old child, all wrinkled, and tangled up in its own shining golden hair and beard. It thanked him kindly enough for freeing it, and asked him what he would like for a gift, a fine wife or a pot of gold. Tom said he didn't care much for either, but the work of the farm was too hard for him and he'd thank the little man for help with his work. 'Now mind you, never thank me,' said the little thing with an ugly look. 'I'll do the work for you and welcome, but if you give me a word of thanks you'll never get a hand's turn more from me. If you want me just call, "Yallery Brown, from out of the mools come to help me", and I'll be there.' And with that he picked a dandelion clock, blew it into Tom's eyes, and was gone.

In the morning Tom found all his work done, and he had no need to do a single stroke. At first he thought he was in Paradise, but after a while things did not go so well, for if his work was done all the other men's work was undone and destroyed, and his fellow workmen began to blame him for it. He thought he would do the work himself, and not be beholden to Yallery Brown, but not a hand's turn could he do, and at last, when the men had complained of him and the master had given him the sack, he called out, 'Yallery Brown, from out of the mools come to me!' Yallery Brown was there on the instant and Tom said to him, 'It's an ill you've done to me and no good. I'll thank you to go away and leave me to work for myself.' At that Yallery Brown burst out laughing, and piped out: 'You've thanked me you fool! You've thanked me and I warned you not. You'll get no more help from me; but if I can't help I'll hinder.' And he burst out singing:

> 'Work as thou will
>   Thou'lt never do well;
> Work as thou may'st
>   Thou'lt never gain grist;
> For harm and mischance and Yallery Brown
> Thou'st let out thyself from under the stone.'

And ever after that nothing went well with poor Tom Tiver, and however he worked he could never do good, and there was ill-fortune on whatever he touched, and till the day of his death Yallery Brown never stopped troubling him.

The Fens

The White Cap

Once there was a boy who wandered away from the right path on a journey to his home, and lost himself in a big wood; night came on, and he lay down tired out, and fell asleep. When he woke, two or three hours after, he could see that a bear was lying beside him, with its head on his little bundle of clothes. It got up, and the boy was very much frightened at first, but, finding the bear was quite tame and gentle, he allowed the animal to lead him out of the wood, to a spot where he could see a light. Walking towards it, he found it came from a little turf hut. In answer to his knock, a little woman opened the door, kindly inviting him to enter. There he saw another little woman sitting by the fire. After a good supper, he was told he must share with them the only bed, and lying down, he fell fast asleep, to be wakened when the clock struck twelve by his bedfellows, who sprang up, putting on little white caps, which hung at the bed's head. One said, 'Here's off,' and the other, 'Here's after,' and they suddenly disappeared, as though flying. Afraid to stay in the hut alone, and seeing another white cap hanging at the bed's head, the boy seized it, saying, 'Here's after.' He was immediately transported to the fairy ring outside the door of the hut where the little women were dancing merrily. Then one said, 'Here's off to a gentleman's house,' and the other, 'Here's after,' so the boy did likewise, and found himself on the top of a tall chimney. The first fairy said, 'Down the chimney,' and the others repeating the usual formula, down they went, first to the kitchen, and then to the cellar. Here they began collecting bottles of wine to take away; they opened one, and gave it to the boy, who drank so greedily that he fell asleep; on waking, he found himself alone, and in fear and trembling, went up to the kitchen, where he met the servants, and was taken before the master of the mansion.

He could give no satisfactory account of himself, and was condemned to be hanged.

On the scaffold he saw, pushing eagerly through the crowd, a little woman carrying a white cap, and wearing a similar one. She asked the judge if the prisoner might be hanged in the cap, and he gave his consent. So she walked up to the scaffold, and placed it on the lad's head, saying, 'Here's off!' He quickly said, 'Here's after!' and away they went like lightning to the turf hut. Here the fairy explained that she had been displeased by his taking the magic cap, and that if befriended by fairies he must in future never take liberties with their property. This he promised, and after a good meal was allowed to depart to his home.

Herefordshire

The Frensham Caldron

The most famous utensil lent by fairies was the Frensham Caldron, mentioned by Aubrey in *The Natural History of Surrey* (vol. III). There was a fairy hill near Frensham, to which everyone who needed an unusually large cooking pot resorted, asked for the loan of the pot, mentioned the need he had of it and the date at which he would return it, on which the pot was handed out to him. Aubrey unfortunately does not mention whether the fairy was invisible or seen. The arrangement worked smoothly until one unpunctual borrower forgot to return the caldron on the specified day. When at length he brought it back it was not accepted, so it was brought back and hung in the vestry of Frensham Church, where it was to be seen in Aubrey's day, though it has since disappeared.

The Doctor and the Fairy Princess

Late one night, so the story goes, a great doctor, who lived near Lough Neagh, was awoke by the sound of a carriage driving up to his door, followed by a loud ring. Hastily throwing on his clothes, the doctor ran down, when he saw a little sprite of a page standing at the carriage door, and a grand gentleman inside.

'Oh, doctor, make haste and come with me,' exclaimed the gentleman. 'Lose no time, for a great lady has been taken ill, and she will have no one to attend her but you. So come along with me at once in the carriage.'

On this the doctor ran up again to finish his dressing, and to put up all that might be wanted, and was down again in a moment.

'Now quick,' said the gentleman, 'you are an excellent good fellow. Sit down here beside me, and do not be alarmed at anything you may see.'

So on they drove like mad – and when they came to the ferry, the doctor thought they would wake up the ferryman and take the boat; but no, in they plunged, carriage and horses, and all, and were at the other side in no time without a drop of water touching them.

Now the doctor began to suspect the company he was in; but he held his peace, and they went on up Shane's Hill, till they stopped at a long, low, black house, which they entered, and passed along a narrow dark passage, groping their way, till, all at once, a bright light lit up the walls, and some attendants having opened a door, the doctor found himself in a gorgeous chamber all hung with silk and gold; and on a silken couch lay a beautiful lady, who exclaimed with the most friendly greeting –

'Oh, doctor, I am so glad to see you. How good of you to come.'

'Many thanks, my lady,' said the doctor, 'I am at your ladyship's service.'

And he stayed with her till a male child was born; but when he looked round there was no nurse, so he wrapped it in swaddling clothes and laid it by the mother.

'Now,' said the lady, 'mind what I tell you. They will try to put a spell on you to keep you here; but take my advice, eat no food and drink no wine, and you will be safe; and mind, also, that you express no surprise at anything you see; and take no more than five golden guineas, though you may be offered fifty or a hundred, as your fee.'

'Thank you, madam,' said the doctor, 'I shall obey you in all things.'

With this the gentleman came into the room, grand and noble as a prince, and then he took up the child, looked at it and laid it again on the bed.

Now there was a large fire in the room, and the gentleman took the fire shovel and drew all the burning coal to the front, leaving a great space at the back of the grate; then he took up the child again and laid it in the hollow at the back of the fire and drew all the coal over it till it was covered; but, mindful of the lady's advice, the doctor said never a word. Then the room suddenly changed to another still more beautiful, where a grand feast was laid out, of all sorts of meats and fair fruits and bright red wine in cups of sparkling crystal.

'Now, doctor,' said the gentleman, 'sit down with us and take what best pleases you.'

'Sir,' said the doctor, 'I have made a vow neither to eat nor drink till I reach my home again. So please let me return without further delay.'

'Certainly,' said the gentleman, 'but first let me pay you for your trouble,' and he laid down a bag of gold on the table and poured out a quantity of bright pieces.

'I shall only take what is my right and no more,' said

the doctor, and he drew over five golden guineas, and placed them in his purse. 'And now, may I have the carriage to convey me back, for it is growing late?'

On this the gentleman laughed. 'You have been learning secrets from my lady,' he said. 'However, you have behaved right well, and you shall be brought back safely.'

So the carriage came, and the doctor took his cane, and was carried back as the first time through the water – horses, carriage, and all – and so on till he reached his home all right just before daybreak. But when he opened his purse to take out the golden guineas, there he saw a splendid diamond ring along with them in the purse worth a king's ransom, and when he examined it he found the two letters of his own name carved inside. So he knew it was meant for him, a present from the fairy prince himself.

All this happened a hundred years ago, but the ring still remains in the doctor's family, handed down from father to son, and it is remarked, that whoever wears it as the owner for the time has good luck and honour and wealth all the days of his life.

'And by the light that shines, this story is true,' added the narrator of the tale, using the strong form of asseveration by which the Irish-speaking peasants emphasize the truth of their words.

Ireland

'I Weat, You Weat'

A farmer in Hampshire was sorely distressed by the unsettling of his barn. However straightly over-night he laid his sheaves on the threshing-floor for the application of the morning's flail, when morning came, all was topsy-turvy, higgledy-piggledy, though the door remained locked, and there was no sign whatever of irregular entry. Resolved to find out who played him these mischievous pranks, Hodge couched himself one night deeply among the sheaves, and watched for the enemy. At length midnight arrived, the barn was illuminated as if by moonbeams of wonderful brightness, and through the key-hole came thousands of elves, the most diminutive that could be imagined. They immediately began their gambols among the straw, which was soon in a most admired disorder. Hodge wondered, but interfered not; but at last the supernatural thieves began to busy themselves in a way still less to his taste, for each elf set about conveying the crop away, a straw at a time, with astonishing activity and perseverance. The keyhole was still their port of egress and regress, and it resembled the aperture of a bee-hive, on a sunny day in June. The farmer was rather annoyed at seeing his grain vanish in this fashion, when one of the fairies said to another in the tiniest voice that ever was heard – '*I weat, you weat.*' Hodge could contain himself no longer. He leaped out crying, 'The devil sweat ye. Let me get among ye!' when they all flew away so frightened that they never disturbed the barn any more.

Hampshire

The Fairy Widower

Not many years since a very pretty girl called Jenny
Permuen lived in Towednack. She was of poor parents,
and lived in service. There was a good deal of romance,
or what the old people called nonsense, in Jenny. She was
always smartly dressed, and she would arrange wild-
flowers very gracefully in her hair. As a consequence,
Jenny attracted much of the attention of the young men,
and again, as a consequence, a great deal of envy from
the young women. Jenny was, no doubt, vain; and her
vanity, which most vain persons will say is not usual, was
accompanied by a considerable amount of weakness on
any point connected with her person. Jenny loved flattery,
and being a poor, uneducated girl, she had not the genius
necessary to disguise her frailty. When any man told her
she was lovely, she quite admitted the truth of the assertion
by her pleased looks. When any woman told her not to
be such a fool as to believe such nonsense, her lips, and
eyes too, seemed to say you are only jealous of me, and
if there was a pool of water near, nature's mirror was

speedily consulted to prove to herself that she was really the best-looking girl in the parish. Well, one day Jenny, who had been for some time out of a situation, was sent by her mother down to the lower parishes to 'look for a place'. Jenny went on merrily enough until she came to the four cross roads on the Lady Downs, when she discovered that she knew not which road to take. She looked first one way and then another, and she felt fairly puzzled, so she sat down on a boulder of granite, and began, in pure want of thought, to break off the beautiful fronds of ferns which grew abundantly around the spot she had chosen. It is hard to say what her intentions were, whether to go on, to return, or to remain where she was, so utterly indifferent did Jenny appear. Some say she was entirely lost in wild dreams of self-glorification. However, she had not sat long on this granite stone, when hearing a voice near her, she turned round and saw a young man.

'Well, young woman,' says he, 'and what are you after?'

'I am after a place, sir,' says she.

'And what kind of a place do you want, my pretty young woman?' says he, with the most winning smile in the world.

'I am not particular, sir,' says Jenny; 'I can make myself generally useful.'

'Indeed,' says the stranger; 'do you think you could look after a widower with one little boy?'

'I am very fond of children,' says Jenny.

'Well, then,' says the widower, 'I wish to hire for a year and a day a young woman of your age, to take charge of my little boy.'

'And where do you live?' inquired Jenny.

'Not far from here,' said the man; 'will you go with me and see?'

'An it please you to show me,' said Jenny.

'But first, Jenny Permuen,' – Jenny stared when she found the stranger knew her name. He was evidently an entire stranger in the parish, and how could he have learnt her name, she thought. So she looked at him somewhat astonished. 'Oh! I see, you suppose I didn't know you; but do you think a young widower could pass through Towednack and not be struck with such a pretty girl? Beside,' he said, 'I watched you one day dressing your hair in one of my ponds, and stealing some of my sweet-scented violets to put in those lovely tresses. Now, Jenny Permuen, will you take the place?'

'For a year and a day?' asked Jenny.

'Yes, and if we are pleased with each other then, we can renew the engagement.'

'Wages,' said Jenny.

The widower rattled the gold in his breeches-pocket.

'Wages! well, whatever you like to ask,' said the man.

Jenny was charmed; all sorts of visions rose before her eyes, and without hesitation she said –

'Well, I'll take the place, sir; when must I come?'

'I require you now – my little boy is very unhappy, and I think you can make him happy again. You'll come at once?'

'But mother' –

'Never mind mother, I'll send word to her.'

'But my clothes' –

'The clothes you have will be all you require, and I'll put you in a much gayer livery soon.'

'Well, then,' says Jenny, ''tis a bargain' –

'Not yet,' says the man; 'I've got a way of my own, and you must swear my oath.'

Jenny looked frightened.

'You need not be alarmed,' said the man, very kindly; 'I only wish you to kiss that fern-leaf which you have in your hand, and say, "For a year and a day I promise to stay."'

'Is that all?' said Jenny; so she kissed the fern-leaf and said –

'For a year and a day
I promise to stay.'

Without another word he walked forward on the road leading eastward. Jenny followed him – she thought it strange that her new master never opened his lips to her all the way, and she grew very tired with walking. Still onward and onward he went, and Jenny was sadly weary and her feet dreadfully sore. At last poor Jenny began to cry. He heard her sob and looked round.

'Tired are you, poor girl? Sit down – sit down,' says the man, and he took her by the hand and led her to a mossy bank. His kindness completely overcame her, and she burst into a flood of tears. He allowed her to cry for a few minutes, then taking a bunch of leaves from the bottom of the bank, he said, 'Now I must dry your eyes, Jenny.'

He passed the bunch of leaves rapidly first over one and then over the other eye.

The tears were gone. Her weariness had departed. She felt herself moving, yet she did not know that she had moved from the bank. The ground appeared to open, and they were passing very rapidly under the earth. At last there was a pause.

'Here we are, Jenny,' said he, 'there is yet a tear of sorrow on your eyelids, and no human tears can enter our homes, let me wipe them away.' Again Jenny's eyes were brushed with the small leaves as before, and, lo! before her was such a country as she had never seen previously. Hill and valley were covered with flowers, strangely varied in colour, but combining into a most harmonious whole; so that the region appeared sown with gems which glittered in a light as brilliant as that of the summer sun, yet as mild as the moonlight. There were rivers clearer than any water she had ever seen on the granite hills, and waterfalls and fountains; while everywhere ladies and gentlemen dressed in green and gold were walking, or sporting, or reposing on banks of flowers, singing songs or telling stories. Oh! it was a beautiful world.

'Here we are at home,' said Jenny's master; and strangely enough he too was changed; he was the most beautiful little man she had ever seen, and he wore a green silken coat covered with ornaments of gold. 'Now,' said he again, 'I must introduce you to your little charge.' He led Jenny into a noble mansion in which all the furniture was of pearl and ivory, inlaid with gold and silver, and studded with emeralds. After passing through many rooms, they came at length to one which was hung all over with lace, as fine as the finest cobweb, most beautifully worked with flowers; and, in the middle of this room was a little cot made out of some beautiful sea-shell, which reflected so many colours that Jenny could scarcely bear to look at it. She was led to the side of this, and she saw, as she said, 'One of God's sweetest angels sleeping there.' The little boy was so beautiful that she was ravished with delight.

'This is your charge,' said the father; 'I am the king in this land, and I have my own reasons for wishing my boy to know something of human nature. Now you have nothing to do but to wash and dress the boy when he wakes, to take him to walk in the garden, and to put him to bed when he is weary.'

Jenny entered on her duties, and gave, and continued to give, satisfaction. She loved the darling little boy, and he appeared to love her, and the time passed away with astonishing rapidity.

Somehow or other she had never thought of her mother. She had never thought of her home at all. She was happy and in luxury, and never reckoned the passing of time.

Howsoever happiness may blind us to the fact, the hours and days move onward. The period for which Jenny had bound herself was gone, and one morning she awoke and all was changed. She was sleeping in her own bed in her mother's cottage. Everything was strange to her, and she appeared strange to everybody. Numerous old gossips were called in to see Jenny, and to all Jenny told her strange tale alike. One day, old Mary Calineck of Zennor came, and she heard, as all the others had done, the story of the widower, and the baby, and the beautiful country. Some of the old crones who were there at the time said the girl was 'gone clean daft'. Mary looked very wise – 'Crook your arm, Jenny,' said she.

Jenny sat up in the bed and bent her arm, resting her hand on her hip.

'Now say, I hope my arm may never come uncrooked if I have told ye a word of a lie.'

'I hope my arm may never come uncrooked if I have told ye a word of a lie,' repeated Jenny.

'Uncrook your arm,' said Mary.

Jenny stretched out her arm.

'It is truth the girl is telling,' said Mary; 'and she has been carried by the small people to some of their countries under the hills.'

'Will the girl ever come right in her mind?' asked her mother.

'All in good time,' said Mary; 'and if she will but be honest, I have no doubt but her master will take care that she never wants.'

Howbeit, Jenny did not get on very well in the world. She married and was discontented and far from happy. Some said she always pined after the fairy widower. Others said they were sure she had misbehaved herself, or she would have brought back lots of gold. If Jenny had not dreamt all this, while she was sitting picking ferns on the granite boulder, she had certainly had a very strange adventure.

Cornwall

Farisees

Keightley in *The Fairy Mythology* (p. 305) quotes Brand in confirmation of 'farisees' as the Suffolk name for fairies. The Suffolk children used to be confused between the farisees and the biblical mentions of the Pharisees. Brand in *Popular Antiquities* (vol. II, p. 503) says:

Not many years ago a butcher near Woodbridge went to a farmer's wife to buy a calf, and finding, as he expressed it, that 'the cratur was all o' a muck' he desired the farmer to hang a flint by a string in the crib, so as to be just clear of the calf's head. 'Becaze,' said he, 'the calf is rid every night by the *farisees*, and the stone will brush them off.'

The Duergar

These are rather vaguely described in *Northumberland Words* as 'the worst and most malicious order of fairies'. In other words, the Unseelie Court, or rather, some obscure members of it, for in the Highlands the sluagh or host makes up the most numerous part of the Unseelie Court. Duergars are the Black dwarfs of the North of England, always full of malice and the enemies of mankind. They are mostly solitary fairies. A representative story about a duergar is told in F. Grice's *Folk-Tales of the North Country*. It is set in the Simonside Hills of Northumberland. A stranger, making his way to Rothbury, lost himself on the hills and was overtaken by darkness. He knew no landmarks to guide him and the ground was very treacherous, so he decided that the only thing to do was to shelter for the night under a rock and wait till morning. But as he came up to the rock he saw a faint light at a little distance, and when he had fumbled his way towards it he found that the light came from a small smouldering fire inside a rough stone hut, such as the shepherds build for shelter. There were two grey stones on each side of the fire, to the right of which was a pile of kindling and to the left two great logs. There was no one there. The traveller went in with a thankful heart, for he might well have died of exposure on the hillside, revived the fire with some of the kindling and sat down on the right-hand stone. He was hardly seated when the door burst open and a strange figure came into the room. He was a dwarf, no higher than the traveller's knee, but broad and strong. His coat was made of lambskin, his trousers and shoes of moleskins, his hat of green moss, decorated with a pheasant's feather. He scowled at the traveller, but said not a word, stumped past him and perched himself on the other stone. The traveller did not dare to speak first, for he guessed that this was a duergar, and bitterly hostile to men. So they sat staring at each other across the fire, which began to die down. It grew bitterly cold, and at last the traveller could bear it no longer, and put some more kindling on the fire. The dwarf looked at him with anger and disdain, leaned back and picked up one of the two great logs. It was twice as long as he was and thicker than his body, but he broke it across his knee as if it had been matchwood and wagged his head at the traveller as much as to say, 'Why can't you do the like?' The fire blazed up for a time, but soon it began to die down. The kindling was all spent. And the dwarf looked at the traveller as if to challenge him to put on the last log. The traveller thought there was some catch in it, and did nothing. The fire faded out and they sat on in cold darkness. Then in the far distance a cock crew and a faint light showed in the sky. At the sound the dwarf vanished, and the hut and fire with him. The traveller was still sitting on his stone, but it was the topmost peak of a steep crag. If he had moved to the left to pick up the log in answer to the duergar's silent challenge, he would have fallen into the deep ravine and there would have been nothing left of him but broken bones.

Northumberland

Sandy Harg's Wife

Alexander Cromek, in his *Remains of Galloway and Nithsdale Song* gives an excellent example of a stock – that is, the replacement of the stolen human being by a piece of wood, given by glamour the appearance of the stolen human. In this story the attempt failed.

Alexander Harg, a cottar, in the parish of New-Abbey, had courted and married a pretty girl, whom the fairies had long attempted to seduce from this world of love and wedlock. A few nights after his marriage, he was standing with a *halve* net, awaiting the approach of the tide. Two old vessels, stranded on the rocks, were visible at mid-water mark, and were reckoned occasional haunts of the fairies, when crossing the mouth of the Nith. In one of these wrecks a loud noise was heard, as of carpenters at work; a hollow voice cried from the other: 'Ho, what're ye doing?' 'I'm making a wife to Sandy Harg!' replied a voice in no mortal accent. The husband, astonished and terrified, throws down his net, hastens home, shuts up every avenue of entrance, and folds his young spouse in his arms. At midnight a gentle rap comes to the door, with a most courteous three-times touch. The young dame starts to get up; the husband holds her in forbidding silence and kindly clasps. A foot is heard to depart, and instantly the cattle low and bellow, ramping as if pulling up their stakes. He clasps his wife more close to his bosom, regardless of her entreaties. The horses, with most frightful neighs, prance, snort, and bound, as if in the midst of flame. She speaks, cries, entreats, and struggles: he will not move, speak, nor quit her. The noise and tumult increases, but with the morning's coming it dies away. The husband leaps up with the dawn, and hurries out to view his premises. A piece of moss-oak, fashioned to the shape and size of his wife, meets his eye, reared against his garden-dyke, and he burns this devilish effigy.

The importance of maintaining silence and a firm grasp in combating fairy enchantments is shown in this story.

Galloway

The Dun Cow of Mac Brandy's Thicket

There was a man called Mackenzie who was one of the tenants of Oonich in Lochaber, and after a time it happened that every night his cattle-fold was broken down and the cattle grazed through his cornfield. He was sure that it was neither the neighbours nor the cattle who were responsible, and concluded that it must be the fairies, so he fetched his brother, the one-eyed ferryman – who had the second sight – to watch with him. Late in the night they heard a sound as of stakes being pulled up, and the one-eyed ferryman, moving quietly towards the far side of the fold, saw a dun, polled cow throwing the stakes aside and butting the cattle to their feet. She then drove them through the broken fence into the cornfield. The one-eyed ferryman followed her silently, and saw her go up to the Fairy Knoll of Derry Mac Brandy. The knoll opened before her and she went in. The ferryman hastened after her in time to stick his dirk into the turf at the door, so that it would not shut. The light streamed out of the knoll and he saw everything. In the centre of the knoll sat a circle of big old grey men round a fire on which a cauldron was burning. By this time the farmer had come up, but could see nothing until he put his foot on his brother's foot and then the whole scene was clear to him, and he was very much alarmed, and wanted to go away. But the Ferryman called out in a loud voice: 'If your dun cow ever troubles Oonich fold again, I will take everything out of the knoll, and throw it out on Rudha na h-Oitire.' With that he pulled out the dirk and the door shut itself. They went down home, and the dun, polled cow never troubled them again.

Inverness

King Herla

Herla was king of the Ancient Britons, and was challenged by another king, a pigmy no bigger than an ape, and of less than half human stature. He rode on a large goat; indeed, he himself might have been compared to Pan. He had a large head, glowing face, and a long red beard, while his breast was conspicuous for a spotted fawnskin which he wore on it. The lower part of his body was rough and hairy, and his legs ended in goats' hooves. He had a private interview with Herla, in which he spoke as follows: 'I am lord over many kings and princes, over a vast and innumerable people. I am their willing messenger to you, although to you I am unknown. Yet I rejoice in the fame which has raised you above other kings, for you are of all men the best, and also closely connected with me both by position and blood. You are worthy of the honour of adorning your marriage with my presence as guest, for the King of France has given you his daughter, and indeed the embassy is arriving here to-day, although all the arrangements have been made without your knowledge. Let there be an everlasting treaty between us, because, first of all, I was present at your marriage, and because you will be at mine on the same day a year hence.' After this speech he turned away, and moving faster even than a tiger, disappeared from his sight. The king, therefore, returned from that spot full of surprise, received the embassy, and assented to their proposals. When the marriage was celebrated, and the king was seated at the customary feast, suddenly, before the first course was served, the pigmy arrived, accompanied by so large a company of dwarfs like himself, that after they had filled all the seats at table, there were more dwarfs outside in tents which they had in a moment put up, than at the feast inside. Instantly there darted out from these tents servants with vessels made out of precious stones, all new and wondrously wrought. They filled the palace and the tents with furniture either made of gold or precious stones. Neither wine nor meat was served in any wooden or silver vessel. The servants were found wherever they were wanted, and served nothing out of the king's or anyone else's stores, but only from their own, which were of quality beyond anyone's thoughts. None of Herla's provisions were used, and his servants sat idle.

The pigmies won universal praise. Their raiment was

gorgeous; for lamps they provided blazing gems; they were never far off when they were wanted, and never too close when not desired. Their king then thus addressed Herla: 'Most excellent King, God be my witness that I am here in accordance with our agreement, at your marriage. If there is anything more that you desire, I will supply it gladly, on the condition that when I demand a return, you will not deny it.' Hereupon, without waiting for an answer he returned to his tent and departed at about cockcrow with his attendants. After a year he suddenly came to Herla and demanded the observance of the treaty. Herla consented, and followed at the dwarf's bidding. They entered a cave in a very high cliff, and after some journeying through the dark, which appeared to be lighted, not by the sun or moon, but by numerous torches, they arrived at the dwarf's palace, a splendid mansion.

There the marriage was celebrated, and the obligations to the dwarf fittingly paid, after which Herla returned home loaded with gifts and offerings, horses, dogs, hawks, and all things pertaining to hunting and falconry. The pigmy guided them down the dark passage, and there gave them a (small) bloodhound (*canem sanguinarium*) small enough to be carried (*portabilem*), then, strictly forbidding any of the king's retinue to dismount until the dog leapt from his carrier, he bade them farewell, and returned home. Soon after, Herla reached the light of day, and having got back to his kingdom again, called an old shepherd and asked for news of his queen, using her name. The shepherd looked at him astonished, and said, 'Lord, I scarcely understand your language, for I am a Saxon, and you a Briton. I have never heard the name of that queen, except in the case of one who they say was Herla's wife, queen of the earliest Britons. He is fabled to have disappeared with a dwarf at this cliff, and never to have been seen on earth again. The Saxons have now held this realm for two hundred years, having driven out the original inhabitants.' The king was astonished, for he imagined that he had been away for three days only. Some of his companions descended from horseback before the dog was released, forgetful of the dwarf's commands, and instantly crumbled to dust. The king then forbade any more of his companions to descend until the dog leapt down. The dog has not leapt down yet. One legend states that Herla for ever wanders on mad journeys with his train, without home or rest.

Herefordshire

Wild Edric

Shropshire men must have been well acquainted with the fairies five hundred years ago. It was reported then, that our famous champion Wild Edric had had an Elf-maiden for his wife. One day, we are told, when he was returning from hunting in the forest of Clun, he lost his way and wandered about till nightfall, alone, save for one young page. At last he saw the lights of a very large house in the distance, towards which he turned his steps, and when he had reached it, he beheld within a large company of noble ladies dancing. They were exceedingly beautiful, taller and larger than women of the human race, and dressed in gracefully-shaped linen garments. They circled round with smooth and easy motion, singing a soft low song of which the hunter could not understand the words. Among them was one maiden who excelled all the others in beauty, at the sight of whom our hero's heart was inflamed with love. Forgetting the fears of enchantment, which at the first moment had seized him, he hurried round the house, seeking an entrance, and having found it, he rushed in, and snatched the maiden who was the object of his passion from her place in the moving circle. The dancers assailed him with teeth and nails, but backed by his page, he escaped at length from their hands, and succeeded in carrying off his fair captive.

For three whole days, not his utmost caresses and persuasions could prevail on her to utter a single word, but on the fourth day she suddenly broke the silence. 'Good luck to you, my dear!' said she, 'and you will be lucky too, and enjoy health and peace and plenty, as long as you do not reproach me on account of my sisters, or the place from which you snatched me away, or anything connected with it. For on the day when you do so you will lose both your bride and your good fortune; and when I am taken away from you, you will pine away quickly to an early death.'

He pledged himself by all that was most sacred to be ever faithful and constant in his love for her: and they were solemnly wedded in the presence of all the nobles from far and near, whom Edric invited to their bridal feast. At that time William the Norman was newly made king of England, who, hearing of this wonder, desired both to see the lady, and to test the truth of the tale; and bade the newly-married pair to London, where he was then holding his court. Thither then they went, and many witnesses from their own country with them, who brought with them the testimony of others who could not present themselves to the king. But the marvellous beauty of the lady was the best of all proofs of her superhuman origin. And the king let them return in peace, wondering greatly.

Many years passed happily by, till one evening Edric returned late from hunting, and could not find his wife. He sought for her and called her for some time in vain. At last she appeared. 'I suppose,' began he, with angry looks, 'it is your sisters who have detained you such a long time, have they not?'

The rest of his upbraiding was addressed to thin air, for the moment her sisters were mentioned she vanished. Edric's grief was overwhelming. He sought the place where he had found her at first, but no tears, no laments of his could call her back. He cried out day and night against his own folly, and pined away and died of sorrow, as his wife had long before foretold.

It is very curious to find that Wild Edric was already the centre of myth and legend within scarcely more than a century of his own lifetime.

Shropshire

The Laird of Balmachie's Wife

In the olden times, when it was the fashion for gentlemen
to wear swords, the Laird of Balmachie went one day to
Dundee, leaving his wife at home ill in bed. Riding home
in the twilight, he had occasion to leave the high road,
and when crossing between some little romantic knolls,
called the Cur-hills, in the neighbourhood of Carlungy,
he encountered a troop of fairies supporting a kind of
litter, upon which some person seemed to be borne. Being
a man of dauntless courage, and, as he said, impelled by
some internal impulse, he pushed his horse close to the
litter, drew his sword, laid it across the vehicle, and in a
firm tone exclaimed:

'In the name of God, release your captive.'

The tiny troop immediately disappeared, dropping the
litter on the ground. The Laird dismounted, and found
that it contained his own wife, dressed in her bedclothes.
Wrapping his coat around her, he placed her on the horse
before him, and, having only a short distance to ride,
arrived safely at home.

Placing her in another room, under the care of an attentive friend, he immediately went to the chamber where he had left his wife in the morning, and there to all appearance she still lay, very sick of a fever. She was fretful, discontented, and complained much of having been neglected in his absence, at all of which the Laird affected great concern, and, pretending much sympathy, insisted upon her rising to have her bed made. She said that she was unable to rise, but her husband was peremptory and having ordered a large wood fire to warm the room, he lifted the impostor from the bed, and bearing her across the floor as if to a chair, which had been previously prepared, he threw her on the fire, from which she bounced like a sky-rocket, and went through the ceiling, and out at the roof of the house, leaving a hole among the slates. He then brought in his own wife, a little recovered from her alarm, who said that some time after sunset, the nurse having left her for the purpose of preparing a little caudle, a multitude of elves came in at the window, thronging like bees from a hive. They filled the room, and having lifted her from the bed, carried her through the window, after which she recollected nothing further, till she saw her husband standing over her on the Cur-hills, at the back of Carlungy. The hole in the roof, by which the female fairy made her escape, was mended, but could never be kept in repair, as a tempest of wind happened always once a year, which uncovered that particular spot, without injuring any other part of the room.

Angus

Elidor and the Golden Ball

A short time before our days, a circumstance worthy of note occurred in these parts, which Elidurus, a priest, most strenuously affirmed had befallen himself. When he was a youth of twelve years, – since, as Solomon says, 'The root of learning is bitter, although the fruit is sweet,' – and was following his literary pursuits, in order to avoid the discipline and frequent stripes inflicted on him by his preceptor, he ran away, and concealed himself under the hollow bank of a river; and, after fasting in that situation for two days, two little men of pygmy stature appeared to him, saying, 'If you will come with us, we will lead you into a country full of delights and sports.' Assenting, and rising up, he followed his guides through a path, at first subterraneous and dark, into a most beautiful country, adorned with rivers and meadows, woods and plains, but obscure, and not illuminated with the full light of the sun. All the days were cloudy, and the nights extremely dark, on account of the absence of the moon and stars. The boy was brought before the king, and introduced to him in the presence of the court; when, having examined him for a long time, he delivered him to his son, who was then a boy. These men were of the smallest stature, but very well proportioned for their size. They were all fair-haired, with luxuriant hair falling over their shoulders, like that of women. They had horses proportioned to themselves, of the size of greyhounds. They neither ate flesh nor fish, but lived on milk diet, made up into messes with saffron. They never took an oath, for they detested nothing so much as lies. As often as they returned from our upper hemisphere, they reprobated our ambition, infidelities, and inconstancies. They had no religious worship, being only, as it seems, strict lovers and reverers of truth.

The boy frequently returned to our hemisphere, sometimes by the way he had first gone, sometimes by another; at first in company with others, and afterwards alone, and confided his secret only to his mother, declaring to her the manners, nature, and state of that people. Being desired by her to bring a present of gold, with which that region abounded, he stole, while at play with the king's son, the golden ball with which he used to divert himself, and brought it to his mother in great haste; and when he reached the door of his father's house, but not unpursued, and was entering it in a great hurry, his foot stumbled on the threshold, and, falling down into the room where his mother was sitting, the two Pygmies seized the ball, which had dropped from his hand, and departed, spitting at and deriding the boy. On recovering from his fall, confounded with shame, and execrating the evil counsel of his mother, he returned by the usual track to the subterraneous road, but found no appearance of any passage, though he searched for it on the banks of the river for nearly the space of a year. Having been brought back by his friends and mother, and restored to his right way of thinking and his literary pursuits, he attained in process of time the rank of priesthood. Whenever David the Second, bishop of St David's, talked to him in his advanced state of life concerning this event, he could never relate the particulars without shedding tears.

He had also a knowledge of the language of that nation, and used to recite words of it he had readily acquired in his younger days. These words, which the bishop often repeated to me, were very conformable to the Greek idiom. When they asked for water, they said, *Udor udorum*, which signifies 'Bring water'; for Udor, in their language, as well as in the Greek, signifies water. When they want salt, they say *Halgein udorum*, 'Bring salt.' Salt is called ἁλς in Greek, and Halen in British; for that language, from the length of time which the Britons (then called Trojans, and afterwards Britons from Brito, their leader) remained in Greece after the destruction of Troy, became, in many instances, similar to the Greek.

Gerald of Wales (Twelfth Century)

The Ellyllon

This is the tale of an unfortunate farmer named Rowli Pugh who seemed to be the butt of misfortune. If blight came anywhere, it fell on his crops; when all other cattle were flourishing, his were ailing. His wife was an invalid with no strength to do anything about the house or farm, and he was thinking sadly one day that he must sell up the farm and leave, when he was accosted by an ellyl who told him not to be troubled any longer, to tell his wife to leave a lighted candle and sweep the fire clean, and the Ellyllon would do the rest. The ellyl was as good as his word. Every night Rowli and Catti went early to bed leaving the coast clear, every night they heard laughter, merriment and bustle below them, and every morning farm stock and farmhouse were in apple-pie order. Rowli and Catti grew strong and sleek and crops and stock prospered. This went on for three years till Catti grew avid for a glimpse of the little people. One night she left her husband sound asleep, tiptoed downstairs and peeped through a crack of the door. There was the merry throng laughing, gambolling, working at top speed. Their merriment was so infectious that Catti burst out laughing too. At once the candle was blown out, there was a cry and a scamper, and all was quiet. The Ellyllon never came back to work at Pugh's Farm, but he had got into the way of prosperity and his ill-fortune did not return.

South Glamorgan

Robin Goodfellow

From Oberon, in fairyland,
  The king of ghosts and shadows there,
Mad Robin, I at his command,
  Am sent to view the night-sports here;
    What revel-rout
    Is kept about
In every corner where I go,
    I will o'ersee,
    And merry be,
And make good sport, with ho, ho, ho!

More swift than lightning can I fly
  About this airy welkin soon,
And, in a minute's space, descry
  Each thing that's done below the moon:
    There's not a hag,
    Nor ghost shall wag,
  Nor cry, ware Goblin! where I go;
    But Robin I

> Their fears will spy,
>   And fear them home, with ho, ho, ho!

If any wanderers I meet,
  That from their night-sport do trudge home,
With counterfeiting voice I greet,
  And cause them on with me to roam;
    Through woods, through lakes,
    Through bogs, through brakes,
  O'er brush and brier, with them I go,
    I call upon
    Them to come on,
  And wend me laughing, ho, ho, ho!

Ben Jonson (1572/3 – 1637)

Anne Jefferies

The affair of Anne Jefferies of St Teath in Cornwall and the fairies caused almost as great a stir, even in the troubled times of the English Civil War, as the notorious case of the Demon Drummer of Tedworth. It is better documented than many other cases, which appeared only in pamphlets. There was even a letter about her in the Clarendon Manuscripts as early as March 1647, and in 1696, while Anne was still alive, Moses Pitt, the son of Anne's old master and mistress, wrote a printed letter to the Bishop of Gloucester in which he gives an account of Anne Jefferies's later life and of his early memories. Moses Pitt was only a boy when Anne, at the age of nineteen, came into service to his parents. In 1645 she fell into a fit, and was ill after it for some time, but when she recovered she declared that she had been carried away by the fairies, and in proof of this she showed strange powers of clairvoyance and could heal by touch. The first she healed was her mistress. After a time, Anne told some of her fairy experiences, and these are retold by Hunt in *Popular*

Romances of the West of England (pp. 127–9), who also summarizes and gives extracts from Moses Pitt's letter in an appendix (pp. 470–71).

Anne was a clever girl, full of enterprise and curiosity, though she never learned to read. Her curiosity was chiefly excited by the stories she had heard of the fairies, and she was always searching for them. It was the tiny fairies of the West Country that she was looking for, and she was often out after sunset turning up the fern leaves and looking into the foxglove bells, singing,

> 'Fairy fair and fairy bright;
> Come and be my chosen sprite.'

And on fine moonlight nights she would roam down the valley, singing,

> 'Moon shines bright, waters run clear,
> I am here, but where's my fairy dear?'

The fairies afterwards told her they heard her well enough, and would run from frond to frond of the fern as she was searching. In the end they decided to show themselves.

Anne was knitting one day in a little arbour just outside the garden gate when she heard a rustling among the branches as if someone was peeping at her. She thought it was her sweetheart and took no notice. There was silence for a while, except for the click of her needles; then the branches rustled again and there was a suppressed laugh. Anne said rather crossly, 'You may stay there till the cuney grows on the gate ere I'll come to 'ee.' Immediately there was a tinkling sound and a ringing, musical laugh. Anne was frightened, for she knew it was not her sweetheart's, but she stayed where she was, and presently she heard the garden gate open and shut gently, and six little men appeared in the arbour. They were very beautiful, all dressed in green and with the brightest of eyes. The grandest of them had a red feather in his cap and spoke to her lovingly. She put her hand down to him. He jumped on to her palm and she lifted him up on to her lap and he clambered up to her bosom and began kissing her neck. She was perfectly charmed with the little gentleman's love-making and sat there in ecstasy until he called his five companions and they swarmed up her skirts and dress and began to kiss her chin and cheeks and lips, and one put his hands over her eyes. She felt a sharp pricking and everything was dark. Then she was lifted into the air and carried she knew not where, until she felt herself set down, and someone said, 'Tear! tear!' Her eyes were opened again and she found herself in a gorgeous fairyland.

She was surrounded by temples and palaces of gold and silver; there were trees covered with fruit and flowers, lakes full of golden and silver fish and bright-coloured birds singing all around. Hundreds of splendidly dressed people were walking in the gardens or dancing and sporting or reposing themselves in flowery arbours. Anne herself was dressed as finely as any of them. To her surprise they seemed no longer small, but of human size. Anne could have stayed forever in that happy place. She was surrounded and courted by her six friends, but the finest of them still made her his prime favourite, and presently they managed to steal away together and were in the height of happiness when there was a clamour, and her five followers broke in on them, followed by an angry crowd. Her lover drew his sword to protect her, but he was wounded and fell at her feet. The fairy who had first blinded her put his hands over her eyes again. She was whirled up into the air with a great humming, and at length regained her sight to find herself lying on the floor of the arbour surrounded by anxious friends.

Anne never revisited Fairyland, but the fairies did not withdraw their favours. They were with her constantly (though no one else could see them), and nourished her with fairy food. Moses Pitt says in his letter:

She forsook eating our victuals, and was fed by these fairies from that harvest time to the next Christmas-day; upon which day she came to our table and said, because it was that day, she would eat some roast beef with us, the which she did – I myself being then at the table.

He adds later that Anne 'gave me a piece of her bread, which I did eat, and I think it was the most delicious bread that ever I did eat, either before or since'.

After her illness, Anne became very fervent in her devotions, though it was the church Prayer Book that she wished to hear, for she was a fervent Episcopalian and all her prophecies were of ultimate victory to the king. People resorted to her for cures from Land's End to London, and her prophecies had great vogue. It was these even more than her dealings with the fairies which caused her to be prosecuted. She was arrested in 1646 at the suit of John Tregeagle, who was to attain a posthumous supernatural reputation as the Demon Tregeagle, some stories of whom Hunt also tells. He committed her to prison and gave orders that she was not to be fed, but she made no complaints and continued in good health. In 1647, the Clarendon Correspondence notes, she is detained in the house of the Mayor of Bodmin and is still not fed. In the end she was released, went into service with a widowed aunt of Moses Pitt and married a labourer named William Warren.

Moses Pitt was a printer in London where he published the letter to the Bishop of Gloucester, and since he could not himself visit Anne Jefferies, he sent an old friend, Mr Humphrey Martin, to whose little daughter Anne had once given a silver cup from the fairies, to confirm her account of her fairy experience. She would tell him nothing. He wrote:

As for Anne Jefferies, I have been with her the greater part of one day, and did read to her all that you wrote to me; but she would not own anything of it, as concerning the fairies, neither of any of the cures that she did. She answered, that if her own father were now alive, she would not discover to him those things which did happen then to her. I asked her the reason why she would not do it; she replied, that if she should discover it to you, that you would make books or ballads of it; and she said she would not have her name spread about the country in books or ballads of such things, if she might have five hundred pounds for it.

Poor Anne had no desire to suffer again the things she had suffered at Justice Tregeagle's hands.

The subject-matter of Anne's delusion, the type of

fairies that occurred to her, are of great interest. In this remote part of Cornwall, not fifty years after the first performance of *A Midsummer Night's Dream*, we have an illiterate country girl building up a courtly Fairyland of diminutive fairies with all the minuteness and amorousness of the fairies in Shakespeare, Drayton and Herrick. It is clear that the poets built on a real country tradition.

Foul-Weather

There was once a king of a far country who had set his heart on building the most beautiful cathedral in his kingdom; he had it all planned, but by the time the foundations were laid all the money in his coffers was exhausted and he could think of no way of finishing it without laying heavy taxes on his people. One day he went out alone on the mountains pondering what he could do, and there he met a strange old man. 'Why art thou so gone into thought?' the old man asked him.

'Why should I not be gone into thought,' answered the king, 'since I have begun a great cathedral and have not money to finish it.'

'Never make lamentation on that account,' said the little man. 'I myself will build thee a right fair church, better than any in the realm, without asking thee for a dime of money.'

'What wilt thou take from me then?' said the king.

'If you can tell me my name by the time the church is built,' said the dwarf, 'I shall do it for nothing; but if you cannot I will take your heart for forfeit.'

The king knew then that the little old man was a gnome of the Mountain, but he thought to himself that he might well be dead before the work was finished, and if his life was gone he would care little what happened to his heart, so he consented.

The cathedral rose as if by magic. No work was done on it by day, but at night swarms of gnomish creatures toiled on it. The king suggested one addition after another, but he had only to suggest it for it to be done next day, until he despaired of delaying it any further. One evening he went out alone up to the mountains, trying to make up something more he could ask for. He wandered about until he came to the mouth of a cave. A prodigious roaring was coming out of it, a gnomish baby yelling and being soothed. As his mother dandled it she sang

'Weep not, weep not my darling boy;
Hush altogether
And then Foul-Weather,
Thy dad, will come
Tomorrow home,
Bringing a king's heart for thy joy
To play withal, a pretty toy.'

Loudly and harshly she sang, but her song was music to

the king, for it told him the name of his adversary. He crept past the cave and ran down the whole way into his city. It was dark by that time and the gnome was up on the topmost spire fixing the gilded weathercock that would complete the building. The king stood and called at the top of his voice: 'Set it straight, Foul-Weather.' At that the gnome fell with a crash straight down from the tower, and was broken into smithereens, as if he had been made of glass. And the weathercock on that great cathedral has been crooked from that day to this.

Cornwall

The Last Word

In dealing with evil spirits and bogles as well as the Devil, it was important to have the last word. The blue men of the Minch are an example of this. They were evil sea-spirits who used to swim out by the Minch (the strip of water between Lewis and the mainland of Scotland), and the captain of the boat had to hold parley with them and get the last word, preferably in rhyme, or they would sink his ship.

The Four-Leafed Clover

A four-leafed clover is regarded as a protection against fairies. It is chiefly used to dissolve glamour in spells cast either by fairies or magicians. The fairy ointment which enabled mortals to see through the glamorous appearance of the fairies was said to be compounded from four-leafed clover. There are various stories of enchantments pierced by someone who is carrying a sprig of the herb unknowingly in a pack of hay or a handful of grasses. An example is one told by Hunt in *Popular Romances of the West of England* (pp. 107–9).

There was a most beautiful cow called Daisy in a farm at West Buriens, who was in milk for long seasons with a splendid quality of milk, but she never let down more than two gallons, then she would prick her ears forward, give a soft low and hold back her milk. One evening a milkmaid was milking the cows in the meadows when this happened. She put a pad of grass on her head to soften the weight of the pail, picked up the pail and started for home. As she crossed the stile she glanced back at Daisy and saw that she was surrounded by fairies, who swarmed over her with little pipkins in their hands. They patted and stroked her, and Daisy was clearly delighted with their company. One rather bigger than the rest, whom she recognized as a pixy by his impudent grin, was lying on his back with his feet in the air, and the others took turns in standing on them to milk the cow. The girl hurried home to tell her mistress, who would not believe her until she had pulled the wad of grass to pieces by the light of the stable lantern and found a four-leafed clover in the heart of it. Then she was convinced, but unfortunately she did not leave well alone. She consulted her mother, who was a witch, about the best way of driving off the fairies. They concocted a brew of brine and stock-fish and painted Daisy's udder with it. That drove off the fairies effectually, but the farm was none the better of it, for Daisy pined for the loss of her friends, dwindled to skin and bone, and gave no milk at all. A similar tale, but without the sad sequel, is told in the Denham Tracts about a milkmaid at Nether Witton.

A secondary use of a four-leafed clover is to grant wishes. This is the use made of it in J. H. Ewing's story 'Amelia and the Dwarfs'. Here Amelia, held prisoner among the fairies, is able to escape when she finds a four-leafed clover during the fairy dance.

The Smallest Fairies

Who knowes, but in the *Braine* may dwel
Little small *Fairies*; who can tell?
And by their severall actions they may make
Those *formes* and *figures*, we for *fancy* take.
And when we sleep, those *Visions*, *dreames* we call,
By *their* industry may be raised all;
And all the *objects*, which through *senses* get,
Within the *Braine* they may in order set.
And some pack up, as *Merchants* do each thing,
Which out sometimes may to the *Memory* bring.
Thus, besides our owne *imaginations*,
Fairies in our *braine* beget *inventions*.
If so, the *eye's* the *sea* they traffick in,
And on *salt watry teares* their ship doth swim.
And if a *teare* doth breake, as it doth fall,
Or wip'd away, they may a *shipwrach* call.

Margaret, Duchess of Newcastle (1623–73)

The Golden-Haired Girl of Unst

There was a girl whose mother had been bewitched by the Trows at the girl's birth, who grew up to be a lovely creature with golden hair of wonderful beauty. It fell in sunny waves about her, and such an unusual mode of wearing it created much wonder. No child or maiden ever permitted her hair to fall as it pleased, except this girl, and folk did say that whenever she tried to bind it to her head the bright locks refused to obey her fingers, but slowly untwined themselves until they became natural ringlets again.

The girl was a sweet singer – and singing is a fairy gift – and she would wander about lilting softly to herself, while neighbours wondered and young men lost their hearts. It was believed that she was under the special care of Trows, for everything seemed to go smooth for her, and her golden hair was called 'the good gift of them that liked her well'. But it happened that a witch began to covet the Trow gift; and one day, when the girl lay down among some hay and went to sleep, the witch cut off her beautiful hair.

The poor young thing returned to her home shorn of her glory, and after that she pined away. The song died from her lips, the light from her eyes.

When she lay dead in her teens, folk said that the golden hair began to grow again, and had grown to all its former beauty ere the coffin lid was closed.

The witch did not triumph, for the Trows took possession of her and punished her as she deserved.

She was compelled to wander about their haunts and live in a strange manner. She was shadowed day and night (she said) by evil fancies. Whenever she tried to sleep the Trows would come and make queer noises so that she could not rest. Eventually she was spirited away altogether!

Shetland

Fairy Song

By the moone we sport and play,
With the night begins our day;
As we daunce, the deaw doth fall;
Trip it little urchins all,
Lightly as the little Bee,
Two by two and three by three:
And about go wee, and about go wee.

Anon

The Green Children

Very curious fairy anecdotes are to be found in the Medieval Chronicles. One of the strangest of them is the account of the Green Children given by both Ralph of Coggeshall and William of Newbridge. Ralph of Coggeshall in the original Latin is to be found in the *Rolls Series*, No. 68. Keightley gives an English translation of it in *The Fairy Mythology* (pp. 281–3):

Another wonderful thing happened in Suffolk, at St Mary's of the Wolf-pits. A boy and his sister were found by the inhabitants of that place near the mouth of a pit which is there, who had the form of all their limbs like to those of other men, but they differed in the colour of their skin from all the people of our habitable world; for the whole surface of their skin was tinged of a green colour. No one could understand their speech. When they were brought as curiosities to the house of a certain knight, Sir Richard de Calne, at Wikes, they wept bitterly. Bread and other victuals were set before them, but they would touch none of them, though they were tormented by great hunger, as the girl afterwards acknowledged. At length, when some beans just cut, with their stalks, were brought into the house, they made signs, with great avidity, that they should be given to them. When they were brought, they opened the stalks instead of the pods, thinking the beans were in the hollow of them; but not finding them there, they began to weep anew. When those who were present saw this, they opened the pods, and showed them the naked beans. They fed on these with great delight, and for a long time tasted no other food. The boy, however, was always languid and depressed, and he died within a short time. The girl enjoyed continual good health; and becoming accustomed to various kinds of food, lost completely that green colour, and gradually recovered the sanguine habit of her entire body. She was afterwards regenerated by the laver of holy baptism, and lived for many years in the service of that knight (as I have frequently heard from him and his family), and was rather loose and wanton in her conduct. Being frequently asked about the people of her country, she asserted that the inhabitants, and all they had in that country, were of a green colour; and that they saw no sun, but enjoyed a degree of light like what is after sunset. Being asked how she came into this country with the aforesaid boy, she replied, that as they were following their flocks, they came to a certain cavern, on entering which they heard a delightful sound of bells; ravished by whose sweetness, they went for a long time wandering on through the cavern, until they came to its mouth. When they came out of it, they were struck senseless by the excessive light of the sun, and the unusual temperature of the air; and they thus lay for a long time. Being terrified by the noise of those who came on them, they wished to fly, but they could not find the entrance of the cavern before they were caught.

William of Newbridge (a monastery in Yorkshire) adds several details to this account. He says that he had not at first believed it, but further investigation convinced him of its truth. The children appeared in King Stephen's reign. He says that the girl called the country St Martin's Land and said that its inhabitants were Christians. It might be noted that green is the Celtic colour of death and that beans are traditionally the food of the dead.

Suffolk

The Fallen Angels in Hell

        they but now who seemd
In bigness to surpass Earths Giant Sons
Now less then smallest Dwarfs, in narrow room
Throng numberless, like that Pigmean Race
Beyond the *Indian* Mount, or Faerie Elves,
Whose midnight Revels, by a Forrest side
Or Fountain some belated Peasant sees,
Or dreams he sees, while over head the Moon
Sits Arbitress, and neerer to the Earth
Wheels her pale course, they on thir mirth & dance
Intent, with jocond Music charm his ear;
At once with joy and fear his heart rebounds.

John Milton (1608–74)

The Miser on the Fairy Gump

The Gump near St Just in Cornwall had been famous as the meeting-place of the small people. Robert Hunt, in *Popular Romances of the West of England* (pp. 98–101), gives a vivid description of a fairy gathering as tiny, bejewelled and courtly as any to be found in the poetry of Herrick or Drayton.

The old people of St Just had long told their children and grandchildren of the great spectacle there, of the music, dancing and feasting. Modest spectators were not punished, and some had even been given tiny but most precious gifts.

There was one old miser, however, who could never hear of riches without desiring them, and on a night of the full harvest moon he set out to see what he could steal. As he began to climb the Gump he heard music all round him, but he could see nothing. As he climbed higher it became louder, and he suddenly realized that it was under his feet, and in a moment the hill burst open and a hideous crowd of spriggans poured out, followed by a great band of musicians and a troop of soldiers. At the same time the whole hillside was lit up; every blade of grass and every furze bush sparkled with jewels. He stared at them greedily, but was disturbed to see that a number of the spriggans were gathering round him like a kind of guard. None of them was higher than his shoestring, however, so he consoled himself by the thought that he could trample them underfoot, and stood his ground. Then out came a great crowd of servants, carrying the riches that he was waiting for, hundreds of tables set out in the finest order with gold and silver plates, and goblets carved out of rubies and diamonds and all varieties of rich food. He was greedily wondering where to pounce when the fairy court came out in their thousands followed by troops of fairy children scattering scented flowers which rooted themselves as they touched the ground, and last of all came the prince and princess, and moved to the high table upon the dais. This was the richest focus of the miser's greed, and, crouching down, he began to creep up behind it to catch the whole brilliant minuscule of jewels and gold and silk under his broad-brimmed hat. He crept up as the fairies moved in ordered companies to do homage to their rulers and to take their proper places at the tables, apparently unconscious of what was overhanging them.

He was so absorbed with his stealth that he never noticed that the spriggans were moving with him and that each one had cast a shining rope around him. At last he was behind the dais and raised himself to his knees with his hat above his head. Then he suddenly saw that every eye in that great assembly was fixed on him. As he paused, a whistle sounded, every light went out and he was jerked sideways by hundreds of thin cords; he heard the whirr of wings and was pierced all over and pinched from head to foot. He lay stretched on his back, pinned to the ground, while the biggest of the spriggans danced on his nose with shouts of laughter. At length the spriggan shouted, 'Away, away! I smell the day!' and disappeared. The miser found himself lying stretched at the foot of the mound covered with dewy cobwebs. He broke through them and managed to stagger to his feet and totter home. It was a long time before he confessed to anyone what happened to him that night.

Cornwall

The Fairy Reproach

'Pinch him, pinch him, blacke and blue,
Sawcie mortalls must not view
What the Queene of Stars is doing,
Nor pry into our Fairy woing.'

John Lyly (?1554–1606)

A *Lepracaun*

Thomas Fitzpatrick, a young farmer of Kildare, was saun-
tering along one holiday when it came into his head to
shake out the hay and bind up the oats, as the weather
looked like changing. As he was doing so he heard a
stump-tapping sound like a stonechat, only it was late in
the season for a stonechat to be calling. So he stole along
to see what it might be, and, peering through the bushes,
he saw a little wee man with a wee leather apron tied
round his waist hammering away fitting a heelpiece to a
little bit of a brogue. Tom knew it was no other than
the Lepracaun. He knew the Lepracaun was the richest
creature in all Fairyland and he knew if he could keep his
eye fixed on him he could force him to give up one at least
of the crocks of gold he had hidden about in the fields.
So he made a sharp pounce on him and held him tight
and threatened him with all the worst things he could
think of unless he showed him where his gold was hidden.
He was so fierce that the little man was quite frightened,
and he said, 'Come along with me and I'll show ye where

it's hidden.' Tom fairly glued his eyes to the little fellow, who directed him through sticks and stones, and up and down and to-fro till they got to a field just covered with bolyawn buies (ragwort). He pointed to a tall one and said: 'Dig under that bolyawn and ye'll get a crock chuck full of golden guineas.' It was a holiday, so Tom hadn't his spade by him, so he tied his red garter round the bolyawn. 'You'll not be wanting me again,' said the Lepracaun. 'No, no,' says Tom. 'Now you've showed it me I'll off away for a spade.' So the Lepracaun melted away like a drop of water in sand. Tom ran for his spade as fast as the wind. He was gone no time at all, but when he got back there was a red garter round every bolyawn in that field.

County Kildare

A Fairy Knoll

There was a woman in Baile Thangusdail, and she was out seeking a couple of calves; and the night and lateness caught her, and there came rain and tempest, and she was seeking shelter. She went to a knoll with the couple of calves, and she was striking a tether-peg into it. The knoll opened. She heard a gleegashing as if a pot-hook were clashing beside a pot. She took wonder, and she stopped striking the tether-peg. A woman put out her head and all above her middle, and she said, 'What business hast thou to be troubling this tulman in which I make my dwelling?' 'I am taking care of this couple of calves, and I am but weak. Where shall I go with them?' 'Thou shalt go with them to that breast down yonder. Thou wilt see a tuft of grass. If thy couple of calves eat that tuft of grass, thou wilt not be a day without a milk cow as long as thou art alive, because thou hast taken my counsel.'

As she said, she never was without a milk cow after that, and she was alive fourscore and fifteen years after the night that was there.

West Highlands

Tom Tit Tot

The Tom Tit Tot story is the liveliest English version of the type that is best known in Grimm's 'Rumpelstiltskin'. Edward Clodd published a monograph, *Tom Tit Tot*, founded on the Suffolk version of the tale, which he reproduced in full. It is one of the best of the English folk-tales, lively in style and dialect, and deserves to be included here in its complete form:

Well, once upon a time there were a woman and she baked five pies. And when they come out of the oven, they was that overbaked, the crust were too hard to eat. So she says to her darter –

'Maw'r,' says she, 'put you them there pies on the shelf an' leave 'em there a little, an' they'll come agin' – she meant, you know, the crust 'ud get soft.

But the gal, she says to herself, 'Well, if they'll come agin, I'll ate 'em now.' And she set to work and ate 'em all, first and last.

Well, come supper time the woman she said, 'Goo you

and git one o' them there pies. I dare say they've come agin now.'

The gal she went an' she looked, and there warn't nothin' but the dishes. So back she come and says she, 'Noo, they ain't come agin.'

'Not none on 'em?' says the mother.

'Not none on 'em,' says she.

'Well, come agin, or not come agin,' says the woman, 'I'll ha' one for supper.'

'But you can't, if they ain't come,' says the gal.

'But I can,' says she. 'Goo you and bring the best of 'em.'

'Best or worst,' says the gal, 'I've ate 'em all, and you can't ha' one till that's come agin.'

Well, the woman she were wholly bate, and she took her spinnin' to the door to spin, and as she span she sang –

> 'My darter ha' ate five, five pies to-day –
> My darter ha' ate five, five pies to-day.'

The king he were a comin' down the street an he hard her sing, but what she sang he couldn't hare, so he stopped and said –

'What were that you was a singun of, maw'r?'

The woman, she were ashamed to let him hare what her darter had been a doin', so she sang, 'stids o' that –

'My darter ha' spun five, five skeins to-day –
My darter ha' spun five, five skeins to-day.'

'S'ars o' mine!' said the king, 'I never heerd tell of any on as could do that.'

Then he said: 'Look you here, I want a wife, and I'll marry your darter. But look you here,' says he, ' 'leven months out o' the year she shall have all the vittles she likes to eat, and all the gownds she likes to git, and all the cumpny she likes to hev; but the last month o' the year she'll ha' to spin five skeins iv'ry day, an' if she doon't, I shall kill her.'

'All right,' says the woman: for she thowt what a grand marriage that was. And as for them five skeins, when te come tew, there'd be plenty o' ways of gettin' out of it, and likeliest, he'd ha' forgot about it.

Well, so they was married. An' for 'leven months the gal had all the vittles she liked to ate, and all the gownds she liked to git, an' all the cumpny she liked to hev.

But when the time was gettin' oover, she began to think about them there skeins an' to wonder if he had 'em in mind. But not one word did he say about 'em, an' she whoolly thowt he'd forgot 'em.

Howsivir, the last day o' the last month, he takes her

to a room she'd niver set eyes on afore. There worn't nothin' in it but a spinnin' wheel and a stool. An' says he, 'Now, me dear, hare yow'll be shut in to-morrow with some vittles and some flax, and if you hain't spun five skeins by the night, yar hid'll goo off.'

An' awa' he went about his business.

Well, she were that frightened. She'd allus been such a gatless mawther, that she didn't se much as know how to spin, an' what were she to dew to-morrer, with no one to come nigh her to help her. She sat down on a stool in the kitchen, and lork! how she did cry!

Howsivir, all on a sudden she hard a sort of a knockin' low down on the door. She upped and oped it, an' what should she see but a small little black thing with a long tail. That looked up at her right kewrious, an' that said –

'What are yew a cryin' for?'

'Wha's that to yew?' says she.

'Niver yew mind,' that said, 'but tell me what you're a cryin' for.'

'That oon't dew me noo good if I dew,' says she.

'Yew doon't know that,' that said, an' twirled that's tail round.

'Well,' says she, 'that oon't dew no harm, if that doon't

dew no good,' and she upped and told about the pies an' the skeins an' everything.

'This is what I'll dew,' says the little black thing: 'I'll come to yar winder iv'ry mornin' an' take the flax an' bring it spun at night.'

'What's your pay?' says she.

That looked out o' the corners o' that's eyes an' that said: 'I'll give you three guesses every night to guess my name, an' if you hain't guessed it afore the month's up, yew shall be mine.'

Well, she thowt she'd be sure to guess that's name afore the month was up. 'All right,' says she, 'I agree.'

'All right,' that says, an' lork! how that twirled that's tail.

Well, the next day, har husband he took her inter the room, an' there was the flax an' the day's vittles.

'Now, there's the flax,' says he, 'an' if that ain't spun up this night off goo yar hid.' An' then he went out an' locked the door.

He'd hardly goon, when there was a knockin' agin the winder.

She upped and she oped it, and there sure enough was the little oo'd thing a settin' on the ledge.

'Where's the flax?' says he.

'Here te be,' says she. And she gonned it to him.

Well, come the evenin', a knockin' come agin to the winder. She upped an' she oped it, and there were the little oo'd thing, with five skeins of flax on his arm.

'Here to be,' says he, an' he gonned it to her.

'Now, what's my name?' says he.

'What, is that Bill?' says she.

'Noo, that ain't,' says he. An' he twirled his tail.

'Is that Ned?' says she.

'Noo, that ain't,' says he. An' he twirled his tail.

'Well, is that Mark?' says she.

'Noo, that ain't,' says he. An' he twirled his tail harder, an' awa' he flew.

Well, when har husban' he come in: there was the five skeins riddy for him. 'I see I shorn't hev for to kill you to-night, me dare,' says he. 'Yew'll hev yar vittles and yar flax in the mornin',' says he, an' away he goes.

Well, ivery day the flax an' the vittles, they was browt, an' ivery day that there little black impet used for to come mornin's and evenin's. An' all the day the mawther she set a tryin' fur to think of names to say to it when te come at night. But she niver hot on the right one. An' as that got to-warts the ind o' the month, the impet that began for to look soo maliceful, an' that twirled that's tail faster an' faster each time she gave a guess.

At last te come to the last day but one. The impet that come at night along o' the five skeins, an' that said –

'What, hain't yew got my name yet?'

'Is that Nicodemus?' says she.

'Noo, t'ain't,' that says.

'Is that Sammle?' says she.

'Noo, t'ain't,' that says.

'A-well, is that Methusalem?' says she.

'Noo, t'aint that norther,' he says.

Then that looks at her with that's eyes like a cool o' fire, an' that says, 'Woman, there's only to-morrer night, an' then yar'll be mine!' An' away te flew.

Well, she felt that horrud. Howsomediver, she hard the king a coming along the passage. In he came, an' when he see the five skeins, he says, says he –

'Well, me dare,' says he, 'I don't see but what yew'll ha' your skeins ready to-morrer night as well, an' as I reckon I shorn't ha' to kill you, I'll ha' supper in here to-night.' So they brought supper, an' another stool for him, and down the tew they sat.

Well, he hadn't eat but a mouthful or so, when he stops and begins to laugh.

'What is it?' says she.

'A-why,' says he, 'I was out a-huntin' to-day, an' I got away to a place in the wood I'd never seen afore. An' there was an old chalk pit. An' I heerd a sort of a hummin', kind o'. So I got off my hobby, an' I went right quiet to the pit, an' I looked down. Well, what should there be but the funniest little black thing yew iver set eyes on. An' what was that a dewin' on, but that had a little spinnin' wheel, an' that were a spinnin' wonnerful fast, an' a twirlin' that's tail. An' as that span, that sang –

"Nimmy nimmy not,
My name's Tom Tit Tot."'

Well, when the mawther heerd this, she fared as if she could ha' jumped outer her skin for joy, but she di'n't say a word.

Next day, that there little thing looked soo maliceful when he come for the flax. An' when night came, she heerd that a knockin' agin the winder panes. She oped the winder, an' that come right in on the ledge. That were grinnin' from are to are, an' Oo! that's tail were twirlin' round so fast.

'What's my name?' that says, as that gonned her the skeins.

'Is that Solomon?' she says, pretendin' to be afeard.

'Noo, t'ain't,' that says, an' that come fudder inter the room.

'Well, is that Zebedee?' says she agin.

'Noo, t'ain't,' says the impet. An' then that laughed an' twirled that's tail till yew cou'n't hardly see it.

'Take time, woman,' that says; 'next guess, an' you're mine.' An' that stretched out that's black hands at her.

Well, she backed a step or two, an' she looked at it, and then she laughed out, an' says she, a pointin' of her finger at it –

> 'Nimmy nimmy not,
> Yar name's Tom Tit Tot.'

Well, when that hard her, that shruck awful an' awa' that flew into the dark, an' she niver saw it noo more.

Suffolk

Taffy ap Sion

Taffy ap Sion stepped one evening into a fairy circle and danced, as he thought, for a few minutes, but when he stepped out everything was changed. He made his way to his old cottage, but it was gone, and a handsome stone farm stood in its place. The farmer heard his story and treated him kindly. He offered him a meal, and promised to take him to see old Catti Shon, the oldest inhabitant, who might remember his name. The farmer led the way, but as he went he heard the footsteps behind him grow lighter and lighter and turned just in time to see Taffy crumble and fall to the ground as a little heap of ashes.

Wales